STERLING BIOGRAPHIES

TECUMSEH

Shooting Star of the Shawnee

Dwight Jon Zimmerman

STERLING

New York / London
www.sterlingpublishing.com/kids

To you, and everyone like you, who enjoys the adventure of reading.
Welcome!

STERLING and the distinctive Sterling logo are registered trademarks of
Sterling Publishing Co., Inc.

Library of Congress Cataloging-in-Publication Data
Zimmerman, Dwight Jon.
  Tecumseh : Shooting Star of the Shawnee / by Dwight Jon Zimmerman.
      p. cm. — (Sterling biographies)
  Includes bibliographical references and index.
  ISBN 978-1-4027-6847-7 (hardcover) — ISBN 978-1-4027-6288-8 (pbk.) 1. Tecumseh,
Shawnee chief, 1768–1813—Juvenile literature. 2. Shawnee Indians—Biography—Juvenile
literature. 3. Shawnee Indians—Wars, 1775–1783—Juvenile literature. I. Title.
  E99.S35T469 2010
  970.004'97—dc22
  [B]

                                                                                           2009024142

Lot#: 10 9 8 7 6 5 4 3 2 1
03/10

Published by Sterling Publishing Co., Inc.
387 Park Avenue South, New York, NY 10016
© 2010 by Dwight Jon Zimmerman

Distributed in Canada by Sterling Publishing
c/o Canadian Manda Group, 165 Dufferin Street
Toronto, Ontario, Canada M6K 3H6
Distributed in the United Kingdom by GMC Distribution Services
Castle Place, 166 High Street, Lewes, East Sussex, England BN7 1XU
Distributed in Australia by Capricorn Link (Australia) Pty. Ltd.
P.O. Box 704, Windsor, NSW 2756, Australia

Sterling ISBN 978-1-4027-6288-8 (paperback)
          ISBN 978-1-4027-6847-7 (hardcover)

Image research by Larry Schwartz

For information about custom editions, special sales, premium and corporate
purchases, please contact Sterling Special Sales Department at 800-805-5489
or specialsales@sterlingpublishing.com.

3 1558 00262 4906

Contents

Events in the Life of Tecumseh

1768

March 1768
Tecumseh is born.

1768
The Treaty of Fort Stanwix is signed, allowing white settlement in Kentucky.

October 10, 1774
Tecumseh's father, Pukeshinwau, is killed in the Battle of Point Pleasant.

April 19, 1775
The Battle of Lexington and Concord launches the American Revolution.

September 3, 1783
The Treaty of Paris, ending the American Revolution, is signed. Great Britain fails to defend the rights of Indians.

1785
The Northwest Indian War, an on-and-off conflict between Native Americans and the United States fought mostly in what is now Ohio, Kentucky, and Tennessee, begins.

January 31, 1786
The Treaty of Fort Finney, transferring Shawnee land in eastern and southern Ohio to the federal government, is signed.

1792
A pan-tribal confederacy led by the Shawnee is formed to stop American westward expansion.

September 30, 1792
Cheeseekau, Tecumseh's oldest brother, is killed in the Battle of Buchanan's Station.

August 3, 1795
The Treaty of Greenville, ending the Northwest Indian War, is signed. Tribes sell large portions of Ohio, and some other territory, to the United States.

August 1794
Tecumseh plays a minor role in the Battle of Fallen Timbers.

1802
Tecumseh begins to lay plans for a new pan-tribal confederacy to protect Indian tribes and land.

June 16, 1806
Tecumseh's brother, the Shawnee Prophet, correctly predicts a solar eclipse. This boosts his reputation and helps bring more followers to Tecumseh.

September 30, 1809
The Treaty of Fort Wayne is signed. Native Americans sell most of Indiana to the United States.

August 12, 1810
Tecumseh meets Indiana Territory governor William Henry Harrison for the first time at Vincennes, Indiana Territory.

November 7, 1811
The Battle of Tippecanoe is fought between warriors led by the Shawnee Prophet and an army led by William Henry Harrison. Though the battle ends in a draw, Harrison claims it as a victory, and the Shawnee Prophet's reputation is ruined.

December 16, 1811
Tecumseh's threat to shake down the houses of tribes who did not join his confederacy comes true when the first of more than two thousand New Madrid earthquakes strikes the Mississippi River valley.

August 15–16, 1812
The Battle of Fort Detroit is fought, ending in a victory for Tecumseh and his British allies.

May 5, 1813
Tecumseh rescues American prisoners from massacre in the Fort Miami incident.

September 10, 1813
The Battle of Lake Erie is fought, ending in an American victory.

October 5, 1813
Tecumseh is killed in the Battle of the Thames.

1813

A Defiant Leader

Now you know how we Indians feel.

In 1810, Tecumseh, a Shawnee chief, was leading a protest against the recently signed Treaty of Fort Wayne. The treaty allowed the United States government to purchase three million acres of tribal land for white settlement. To stop the protests, William Henry Harrison, the governor of Indiana Territory, called Tecumseh and other chiefs together for a council. Though their first meeting, on August 12, had not ended well, Tecumseh had agreed to a second meeting later in the month, on August 20.

The two met by a grove near the governor's home in Vincennes, Indiana Territory. Governor Harrison ordered that a bench be placed on the ground between them. He sat down and motioned for Tecumseh to sit beside him.

As Harrison began talking through an interpreter, Tecumseh slid so that their bodies touched. The governor edged away. Tecumseh moved so that their bodies again touched. The governor slid down the bench. Tecumseh followed. This process continued until the governor protested that he had no more room. When the interpreter told this to Tecumseh, the chief laughed and said, "Now you know how we Indians feel."

When the meeting ended without a resolution, Harrison realized that he faced a new type of chief—one who had a clear and unshakable goal: protecting Native American rights. And not even the great power of the United States' government would scare him.

CHAPTER 1

A Shooting Star Is Born

Preserve . . . the dignity and honor of [the] family [and] . . . lead forth to battle [your] younger brothers.

—Pukeshinwau to Tecumseh's older brother

It was night. Because it was March and the sky was clear, the air was cold and still around the small campsite of the Kispokotha band—a division of the great Shawnee nation. The leader of the band was Pukeshinwau, a war chief. On this quiet night, his attention was focused on a nearby small hut. The only sounds that occasionally broke the evening silence were the cries that came from Pukeshinwau's wife, Methoataaskee. Earlier that day she had gone into labor. A birthing hut was quickly constructed. It was dark before everything was ready for her. Then, as she and her **midwives** approached the hut, a blazing meteor appeared. For a moment, everyone stopped and stared up at the shooting star as it streaked across the sky. When it vanished, Methoataaskee entered the hut and a midwife closed the entrance flap behind them.

The land where the Shawnee lived—which would later become the states of Ohio and Kentucky—was a paradise. The forests were rich with game that could be hunted for food, clothing, and shelter. The soil was fertile and produced a bounty of crops—corn, squash, beans, and other vegetables—and nuts, berries, and other fruits grew wild in abundance.

This photograph shows a meteor streaking across the night sky. Native Americans believed that celestial phenomena such as meteors, also known as shooting stars, were important signs from the spirit world.

Even as he waited for the birth of their new child, Pukeshinwau was troubled and had many things to think about. Earlier his village had received the call to assemble a grand council in Chillicothe, which was located on the Scioto River in south-central Ohio. As one of the most respected war chiefs within the Kispokotha band, Pukeshinwau gathered a group of village leaders and warriors to go with him to the council. His four children were a part of that group, including his oldest child—his son Cheeseekau—and his oldest daughter, Tecumapese. Though his wife was pregnant and due to give birth any day, Methoataaskee also chose to go.

Chillicothe was a four-day journey from their village. On the third day, Methoataaskee went into labor. Later that evening, their fifth child, a boy, was born. Ultimately the couple would have eight children. One died before its first birthday, and nearly nothing is known of three of the siblings. Of the other four, three would make minor marks in history. It was this newborn child who would become legendary as a great Native American patriot. His name was Tecumseh, which meant "Shooting Star."

A Troublesome Situation

The year was 1768, and grand councils were called only when a decision had to be reached on a matter affecting the whole tribe. That the summons was made in March, when travel by a group of any size is difficult, emphasized its urgency and importance. Pukeshinwau's heart was heavy because once he arrived at Chillicothe, he would help decide whether the red tomahawk of war should be passed through the Shawnee villages. This would call for war against the white colonists and the British soldiers, whom the Indians called Long Knives because of the long swords that the officers carried.

To the Shawnee, individual white trappers and traders were no major threat to them and other tribes on the western side of the mountains. In fact, the traders' iron utensils and tools, cloth of linen and cotton, colorful beads, firearms, and other goods had done much to improve Shawnee life, as it had for the other tribes.

But this contact with the whites also threatened the Indian way of life.

Native Americans referred to both British and American soldiers as Long Knives because of the swords they carried. In this c. 1910 painting of a scene from the American Revolution, officers with swords conduct a drill of frontier militia.

The suffering and death among Indian tribes caused by white men's diseases such as smallpox is tragically revealed in this 1853 engraving.

Traders' tools, cloth, and beads were better than those made and fashioned by the Indians. As the old ways of making things were forgotten and lost, the tribes became more dependent upon a steady flow of trader goods. Contact with the white men also brought deadly diseases such as smallpox and measles. Because Indians lacked immunity to these diseases from Europe, outbreaks turned into plagues that traveled from village to village, killing many. And not all trade items were beneficial. Trader alcohol, usually rum, turned too

Indians vs. Native Americans

When explorer Christopher Columbus landed on the island of Hispaniola in 1492, he called the natives he found there "Indians." This was because he thought he had reached the Indies. But he had miscalculated—by about 8,000 miles. Instead, he had discovered what was soon identified as the "New World." The mistaken name for the native peoples, however, remained and came to be used to describe all the native people in North and South America. Today, some native people prefer the term "Native Americans," while others prefer to be called "American Indians." In this book, "Indian" is often used because of its historical accuracy.

Shown are some of the instruments used by surveyors in the 1700s to map the frontier and to set boundaries of Native American land.

many good warriors into lazy men and abusive husbands and fathers. As bad as these ills were, however, they were nothing compared to the threat posed by whites who came after the traders.

First came soldiers who built forts. Behind them came **surveyors** with strange tools that they said would set boundaries—even though no one could see them—that were more unchangeable than a boundary made by a river. Finally there came the settlers. They cleared land, killed wildlife, and constructed buildings and fences on acreage in Kentucky Territory, which they claimed was now theirs. They said they had purchased it from their government, and that their government had bought the land fair and square from the Iroquois Indians who owned it.

To the Shawnee and other tribes living in the region, these claims were ridiculous. The Iroquois, who lived in northeast Pennsylvania and New York, had never lived in Ohio and Kentucky and had no hereditary claim to the land. Yet in the Treaty of Fort Stanwix, signed in New York in 1768, the Iroquois had sold to the British colonial government of Virginia land in Kentucky that was not theirs—and they kept the money for themselves.

It was wrong. But it was done. Now the Shawnee had to decide what they would do.

This is the last page of the Treaty of Fort Stanwix. Next to many of the signatures are animal symbols indicating the names of the Iroquois chiefs who signed the document and sold land they did not own to the British government.

War Council

By tradition, each of the five bands or divisions in the Shawnee nation—the Thawegila, Chalahgawtha, Maykujay, Piqua, and Kispokotha—sometimes also called the Shawnee **confederacy**, held specific duties and responsibilities. The Thawegila and Chalahgawtha bands provided the leadership for the nation. The Maykujays served as priests, medicine men, and counselors. The Piquas maintained tribal traditions such as religious celebrations and the individual responsibilities of men and women. The Kispokothas were responsible for providing leadership in war.

The Shawnee Confederacy

The Shawnee confederacy was made up of five bands, or divisions, of Native Americans that shared the same language and customs. The Shawnee originally lived along the Ohio River valley and as far east as western Maryland. Membership in a band was determined by the father, and even though Shawnee could marry individuals from other divisions, a Shawnee remained a member of his birth band for life. Shawnee men were hunters and warriors. Shawnee women were responsible for farming and child care. Both men and women participated in the education and training of children. Shawnee lived in wigwams, round dwellings made of animal skins that could be quickly built or packed away. The Shawnee had a rich culture and were famous for their excellent beadwork, pottery, and wood carving. When the Shawnee lived in the Ohio region, they were **nomadic**. That changed when they were moved to Oklahoma, originally known as Indian Territory, by the United States government in the mid-1800s.

The Shawnee people often lived in round wigwams covered in animal skins. This 1754 drawing depicts a similar type of wigwam built by Winnebago Indians of Wisconsin.

Pukeshinwau led his group into Chillicothe the day after the birth of Tecumseh. While Tecumseh's mother devoted herself to caring for her new baby and their other children, Tecumseh's father sat in council. The discussions and arguments were many and heated. Though the Shawnee resented what was happening, many did not want to fight. They respected the power of the muskets and cannons of the British military.

The Shawnee chiefs decided it was easier to move away than fight. Land was plentiful, and the chiefs reasoned that if they moved their villages far enough from the settlers, the few settlers would not bother them. When the British government agreed to stop

British soldiers were called redcoats because of the red uniform jackets they wore. This engraving shows a typical "redcoat" uniform of a British foot soldier in the 1700s.

further white settlement in Shawnee homelands in the Ohio River valley, it seemed that a solution had been reached. But white settlers found ways to get around the government's laws. The uneasy peace continued for several years, disrupted by incidents in which individual Shawnee warriors attacked and killed isolated white settlers.

Though the Shawnee resented what was happening, many did not want to fight.

Lord Dunmore's War

Matters finally came to a head in 1774. A series of incidents in which whites and Shawnee were killed gave Virginia colonial governor John Murray, Earl of Dunmore, the excuse he needed to launch a military expedition against the Shawnee living along the Scioto River. The climax of his plan called for an army led by Colonel Andrew Lewis to travel down the Kanawha River, in what is now West Virginia, while another army, led by Lord Dunmore, traveled south down the Ohio River from Fort Pitt (Pittsburgh). Both would rendezvous where the Ohio River joined the Scioto River. Their combined force would then crush the Shawnee.

Lord Dunmore did little to keep his plan secret. As a result, traders and Native Americans in the region who saw the military preparations passed their observations to the Shawnee. When news of Lord Dunmore's plan reached them, the Shawnee chiefs and elders gathered for a grand council. Though outnumbered and outgunned, the chiefs decided they must go to war. Cornstalk, the senior war chief of the Shawnee, ordered the red tomahawk to be passed from village to village.

Chief Cornstalk was one of the most important Shawnee chiefs in the late 1700s. This is a photograph of his statue located on the Point Pleasant battlefield.

Death of a Chief

Tecumseh, now around six years old, watched as his father made the necessary preparations to go into battle. Warriors covered in war paint and wearing eagle feathers danced war dances, performed purification ceremonies in which they drank special vegetable broths, and called upon spirits to aid them in battle. Medicine men performed similar ceremonies. Finally, amid much shouting and ceremonial gunfire, the warriors lined up

Indian warriors going to war often took along sacred bundles to help them communicate with spirits. In this photograph, a Hidatsa Indian holds a bowl of incense over a sacred medicine bundle.

behind Pukeshinwau and, singing their war songs, went off to fight. With them went a sacred bundle needed to summon additional spiritual help just before the battle was joined. These bundles contained a variety of objects and could include such things as special rocks, slivers of wood, animal bones, feathers, and even weapons.

On October 10, 1774, the Shawnee attacked Colonel Lewis's army of about eleven hundred men at Point Pleasant at the mouth of the Kanawha River. The battle lasted most of the day. The Shawnee fought with great skill and courage. One of the warriors was Tecumseh's older brother, Cheeseekau. Despite repeated assaults and suffering approximately two hundred **casualties**, Colonel Lewis's men held their ground. When night fell, Cornstalk ordered his warriors to leave the battlefield.

The exact number of Shawnee warriors killed is unknown, but one who did fall in battle was Pukeshinwau. Cheeseekau reached his dying father in time for Pukeshinwau to tell him "to preserve . . . the dignity and honor" of the family and "lead forth to battle his younger brothers." Then Pukeshinwau died.

Cheeseekau returned to the Scioto, full of grief and aware that, at age thirteen, he was now the head of the family.

Chiefs

Leadership among the Shawnee and other Native Americans was held by individuals who, through their wisdom, abilities, and achievements, were known as chiefs. For men, the fastest way to become a chief was to become a respected warrior. The Shawnee had two types of chiefs, war chiefs and civil chiefs, and men and women could hold positions in both. Civil chiefs were responsible for the many social, agricultural, and religious issues affecting Shawnee life. Because tribal culture gave everyone an equal vote in affairs that affected the tribe, the power of a chief rested in his individual ability or personality. A chief did not possess the same sort of authority that members of the U.S. government and military did. This difference led to many misunderstandings between Indians and the United States.

This 19th-century engraving of the Shawnee chief Kish-Kal-Wa shows the typical ornamentation that was in fashion among the Shawnee.

CHAPTER 2

Time of the American Revolution

Tecumseh . . . [was] proud, courageous and high spirited.

—Stephen Ruddell

News of Pukeshinwau's death caused Tecumseh's family to go into mourning following a ceremony of dances, songs, and speeches that honored the fallen chief. That period of mourning ended after twelve days for everyone except Methoataaskee. Because she was Pukeshinwau's widow, Methoataaskee was obligated by custom to mourn for a year. This meant she had to avoid contact with others in the village, could not smile or laugh, had to wear plain clothes, and could not wash her hands or face. Her period of mourning was complicated by the fact she was once again pregnant. Though she would not know it until they were born, she was carrying triplets.

Though times were difficult, young Tecumseh managed to enjoy

A grieving widow watches over the weapons of her deceased husband, a chief, in this 1785 painting. Each tribe had different customs regarding mourning periods. For the Shawnee, the mourning period for a widow was one year.

life. He was a natural leader and was frequently the organizer of games with other kids. Wrestling and foot races were among his favorites. He was also mischievous, and enjoyed playing tricks and practical jokes that occasionally got him into trouble with his mother.

One of the big influences on his life during this time was his older sister Tecumapese, who became deeply involved in Tecumseh's upbringing. Normally, Pukeshinwau would have been Tecumseh's trainer and teacher. But with Pukeshinwau's passing, and Cheeseekau so young, responsibilities were divided between Cheeseekau and Tecumapese.

Learning the Way of the Shawnee

Tecumapese encouraged Tecumseh to develop good character and to always have high morals. She taught him to respect the old, crippled, and weak members of the tribe, to help them when they needed assistance, and to listen to them in order to gain wisdom from their greater experience. She also taught him respect for authority and a distaste for cruelty.

Cheeseekau was responsible for teaching his younger brother the lore and traditions of Shawnee life and the skills he would need to become a respected member of the tribe. It was a daunting task, because Cheeseekau was just learning these things himself when their father was killed. But their shared tragedy inspired a special bond between the brothers. Cheeseekau taught Tecumseh how to fashion and shoot a bow and arrow, how to fish, and how to stalk and hunt deer, rabbit, ducks, geese, turkey, and other game animals. Tecumseh proved to be a quick study.

Because the Shawnee did not have a written language, Cheeseekau passed all this information by word of mouth. He repeated the stories and lessons to Tecumseh. The younger

In many Native American tribes, the parents were the primary instructors of their children. Men would teach their sons how to hunt and, as seen in this photograph, use weapons such as the bow and arrow.

brother then repeated them word for word until he had committed them to memory.

Like other tribes with an oral tradition, the Shawnee placed great importance on speaking well in front of an audience. The most respected chiefs were almost always great public speakers. Cheeseekau taught Tecumseh how to express himself before individuals and groups. He also taught him how to recognize the subtle and unspoken physical signs and expressions of others, such as when someone refuses to meet a gaze, nervous movements of hands and feet, slouching, and other body movements that reveal truths that spoken words try to hide.

The Vision Quest

Cheeseekau also prepared Tecumseh for his rite of passage into manhood known as the vision quest. The Shawnee believed that their world was filled with spirits that controlled all things and that each person had a protective guardian spirit. For boys, the identity of that guardian spirit was revealed only after he reached puberty and after he had completed a vision-quest ritual that included fasting, meditation, and prayer.

Tecumseh's vision quest began with the ceremonial blackening of his face with paint or ashes, signifying that his fasting had begun. Then, each day for several days, Cheeseekau would take Tecumseh into the woods and leave him alone to meditate. The first session was short—only a few hours. Each later session became longer and longer until his guardian spirit revealed itself to him and his vision quest was complete.

The recipient was forbidden to give details of what was revealed to him because if he did, the power of the guardian spirit would vanish; thus, no details of Tecumseh's vision are known. It is assumed that the vision occurs during a dream or when the individual is in a trancelike state. Several days after his vision quest had begun, Tecumseh informed Cheeseekau that he had his revelation. Tecumseh's face was then washed so that everyone in the tribe would know that his quest had been successful.

Native Americans in the American Revolution

In 1775, the thirteen colonies rebelled against the mother country of Great Britain and the American Revolution began. Almost immediately the Indian tribes and nations became **pawns** in the war between the whites. The British redcoats and the American colonists sought either Indian alliances or Indian **neutrality**.

Though the main fighting occurred within the thirteen colonies, a number of battles happened in the **frontiers** of the Northwest Territory, Kentucky, and Tennessee. These battles were fought between small groups of American troops and Native American tribes supported by the British. Most of the battles were actually Indian raids on white settlements. The worst year of fighting was 1782, known as the "Year of Blood" because so many people—soldiers, warriors, and civilians— were killed.

One of the most important frontier settlements during the American Revolution was Boonesborough, Kentucky, named after the famous frontiersman Daniel Boone. This 19th-century engraving depicts an Indian attack on the settlement's fort.

Though he was too young to fight, Tecumseh regularly saw warriors prepare themselves for war. Upon the war party's return, he and other members of the village celebrated their victories and shared in the grief over those who had fallen.

Sometimes the warriors returned with prisoners. These prisoners were considered the property of their captors, who had sole authority over the prisoners' fates. Those whose faces were painted red were spared their lives and either adopted into the tribe or **ransomed**. Those whose faces were painted black were condemned to death. Standards of the day dictated the decision: Women and children were most often spared, while men of warrior age were most often condemned to death. One such captive adopted into the tribe was twelve-year-old Stephen

The American Revolution (1775–1783)

Also known as the War of Independence, the American Revolution was the conflict by which the thirteen colonies broke free of their mother country, Great Britain. Parliament (the British government) decided to impose a series of taxes on the colonies without consulting the colonists first. The colonies rebelled against Parliament's decision, and so began the war.

In April 1775, the first shots were fired at the Battle of Lexington and Concord. The colonies quickly formed the Continental army headed by General George Washington. A formal declaration of colonies' independence was issued in July 1776.

After eight years of fighting, Great Britain finally signed the Treaty of Paris in 1783, which ended the American Revolution and recognized the United States as an independent country.

This 1863 engraving depicts a moment during the Battle of Lexington and Concord—the first battle fought in the American Revolution between British soldiers and Massachusetts citizen-soldiers known as minutemen.

Ruddell, who was given the name Sinnamatha—"Big Fish."
Because they were close in age and had similar personalities,
he and Tecumseh soon became
inseparable companions. Ruddell
later recalled, "Tecumseh . . .
[was] proud, courageous and
high spirited."

*Though he was too young
to fight, Tecumseh regularly
saw warriors prepare
themselves for war.*

The tribes suffered from
a chronic shortage of guns, gunpowder, and ammunition. Despite
these handicaps, however, they managed to win more battles than
they lost. Thus, it came as a great surprise to the tribes in the West
(who often fought for the British) when, in 1783, Great Britain
surrendered. The British leadership in North America promised
their Indian allies that the British would protect their rights in the
peace treaty that would be signed with the new United States.
Trusting the British, the tribes did not send any representatives.
But those promises proved false.
British negotiators at the bargaining
table ignored the rights of their
allies. The terms of the Treaty of
Paris that ended the war transferred
control of almost all land east of the
Mississippi River and south of the
Great Lakes to American control
without any safeguards to protect
the tribes living there.

This is the signature page of the Treaty of Paris
of 1783 that ended the American Revolution.
The signatures from left to right are those of
British delegate David Hartley followed by
American delegates John Adams, Benjamin
Franklin, and John Jay.

A Pan-Tribal Confederacy

The new American government moved swiftly to establish control. The huge frontier represented an irresistible opportunity to a growing white population hungry for land and to a federal government starved for cash. War veterans received compensation in the form of grants of land. The government also sold large sections to speculators who subdivided and resold the land for huge profits. Before 1783 ended, a steady stream of settlers had crossed the Appalachian and Allegheny mountains and settled in the eastern sections of what is now Ohio, Kentucky, and Tennessee.

Anger over this invasion caused a number of chiefs to call for a **pan-tribal** confederacy to present a united front designed to stop the flow of whites. One of the main leaders was the Mohawk chief Joseph Brant of the Iroquois confederacy, who had fought against the Americans during the Revolution.

To counter unjust actions—such as the recent sale of Shawnee land by the Iroquois—the main belief of this pan-tribal movement was that the land the tribes lived on belonged to *all* the Indians collectively. It could be sold only if all the tribes consented.

Despite bold words and the general agreement among the tribes, the confederacy was fragile. American **commissioners** knew this and cunningly

Artist George Caleb Bingham's 1851 painting symbolized the hopeful frontier spirit American settlers had as they entered the wilderness. Unfortunately, American and Indian civilizations were so different that peaceful accommodation between the two would prove difficult, if not impossible.

The Iroquois confederacy was one of the largest in the Northeast. It was also known as the Five Nations because its members were the Cayuga, Mohawk, Oneida, Onondaga, and Seneca Indian nations. This c. 1570 French engraving shows the chiefs in council reciting the laws of the confederacy.

decided to exploit and intimidate the individual tribes into giving up their lands. In a classic divide-and-conquer strategy, the commissioners began with the most vulnerable tribes. The first group to back down was the Iroquois—Chief Brant's own people. In 1784 at Fort Stanwix, they signed a treaty that surrendered their claims to the upper Ohio River valley region. In January 1785 at Fort McIntosh in Pennsylvania, the American officials forced the Wyandot, Delaware, Ottawa, and Ojibwa tribes to sign a treaty that gave away their territory in eastern and southern Ohio, including land where the Shawnee lived. The American commissioners then focused on the only tribe left— the Shawnee.

By this time, Tecumseh was in his mid-teens and, according to Shawnee custom, a man. But he was still very young and had to remain on the sidelines, a witness to the events occurring around him. That would soon change.

CHAPTER 3

Young Hunter and Warrior

*[Tecumseh] was a man of great courage
and conduct.*

—*Stephen Ruddell*

The American commissioners issued a summons to the
Shawnee leaders, telling them to attend a conference in
January 1786 at Fort Finney, located at the mouth of the
Great Miami River in Ohio. Despite the hazards and
difficulties in traveling through the frontier during the
winter, about 230 Shawnee chiefs and warriors arrived at
Fort Finney on time. They were led by an elderly chief
named Moluntha, who along with the other Shawnee
thought they could shrewdly negotiate and in the end
preserve their land. They were wrong. The commissioners
bluntly told them, "This country belongs to the United
States." The Americans kept up the pressure, refusing
to negotiate any terms. Finally, on January 31, 1786,
Moluntha and the other chiefs bowed their heads and
reluctantly signed the Treaty of Fort Finney, which
surrendered to the federal government most of eastern and
southern Ohio—almost the entire Shawnee homeland.

The American commissioners left, satisfied that they
had firmly established their government's claim on the
Ohio frontier. They were mistaken. Instead, they had
provoked a war.

The commissioners failed to recognize that though the
chiefs represented the Shawnee nation, real authority for

In this 20th-century illustration by Hal Sherman, American delegates present their terms for the Treaty of Fort Finney. The Shawnee people became so angry over the loss of their land that they chose to go to war.

any decision affecting the nation as a whole rested with *all* the members of the tribe. Agreements could have authority only if a large majority agreed to the decision. When Moluntha and the others returned to their villages and reported what had happened, the rest of the Shawnee nation angrily rejected the treaty outright and prepared for war. In addition, they sent messages to nearby tribes in the West, inviting the tribes to join in their war against the United States.

News of the Shawnee plans quickly reached the whites living in Kentucky. As they would be the first to suffer from Indian attack, they decided to strike before the Shawnee did. An eight-hundred-man mounted militia under the leadership of Benjamin Logan was organized, and an offensive campaign against the Shawnee was launched.

A Cold-Blooded Murder

On October 6, 1786, the military unit reached their first objective: the Shawnee village of Mackachack, where Moluntha lived. Even though most Shawnee were going to war, Moluntha and his division of the Shawnee, the Mekoche, remained neutral and continued to advocate peace.

The Kentuckians did not care. To them, all Indians were hostile. They attacked. As it turned out, most of the people of the village were away that day. The fighting was brief, and prisoners, including Moluntha, were quickly rounded up. Moluntha was roughly pulled aside and interrogated. The Kentuckians wanted to find out where the warriors were hiding. At one point, the hotheaded officer who was leading the questioning raised his tomahawk and, because he was angry over attacks committed by other Indians, smashed it into the Shawnee chief's skull, killing him. The officer then scalped the dead chief, intending to keep the scalp as a trophy.

News of the brutal execution swept through all the Indian villages in the region. Even those who still wanted peace agreed that if a white man could murder a helpless old man who sought

Here, artist Hal Sherman illustrates the brutal murder of Shawnee Chief Moluntha, one of the few Shawnee leaders who wished to have peace with the Americans.

peace, the tribes had no choice but to go to war. Logan's force, which held a number of Shawnee captives, was heading back to Kentucky. Meanwhile, the Shawnee began forming war parties to harass Logan's force. Cheeseekau, now a respected war chief, was a leader of one of the parties. Among the nine warriors he chose for his group was Tecumseh, now eighteen years old.

Tecumseh's First Battle

When Tecumseh learned that Cheeseekau agreed to take him on the raid, he began making his preparations. He carried out the required purification rituals that included drinking special herbal broths and performing his war dance. As he did not yet have a firearm, he carefully chose his best arrows and the strongest **gut** for his bowstring. Cheeseekau led his small group of mounted warriors on a raid of revenge. All were well armed. Most had muskets, knives, and tomahawks. Some, like Tecumseh, had only bows and arrows and war clubs.

This 1848 portrait of Tecumseh was based on an 1808 sketch made from life. Though it shows him wearing the chest medal given to him by the British, it erroneously has him in a British general's uniform. For years it was mistakenly believed that the British had made Tecumseh a general.

They had traveled for about three days when Cheeseekau, in the lead, saw a canoe half hidden in the reeds along a riverbank. From its construction, he knew the canoe belonged to a white man. As he turned to alert the rest of his group, a shot rang out and Cheeseekau was knocked off his horse. Immediately the other warriors leaped off their mounts and took cover in the tall grass while their panic-stricken horses galloped away.

The suddenness of the ambush caught Tecumseh unprepared, and he fell off his horse and lost his weapons. As he picked himself up off the ground, he saw the apparently lifeless body of his brother and the blood pouring from a wound in his chest. Tecumseh panicked and ran away from the battlefield. A gunfire exchange between the advancing Shawnee warriors and white ambushers spurred him on. After running a short distance, he ducked behind a fallen tree to catch his breath. He heard more gunshots and the war whoops of his fellow warriors. Though still very much afraid, Tecumseh began crawling back toward the battleground. He wanted to carry away the fallen body of his brother, whom he thought dead.

When he arrived at Cheeseekau's side, Tecumseh was overjoyed to discover that his brother was still alive. Carefully he dragged his brother away. He had

He wanted to carry away the fallen body of his brother, whom he thought dead.

reached the riverbank when the other warriors returned. Their counterattack had been a success. All three of the white men had been killed. By this time, Cheeseekau had fully regained consciousness. Tecumseh was filled with shame. He had allowed fear to overcome him. The others were quick to reassure him. All had known fear. And they pointed out that he had returned to rescue his brother, an important act of courage since he did not know how the battle was going at that time.

Because Cheeseekau's wound was serious, the group retrieved their horses and began the ride back to their village. Only partially soothed by his fellow warriors' reassurances, Tecumseh silently vowed that never again would he run away from an enemy.

Compassion for Prisoners

Tecumseh learned quickly how to fight. Two years later he distinguished himself in a large raid containing more than a hundred warriors, including Tecumseh's friend, Stephen Ruddell, the white boy who had been adopted by the Shawnee. Ruddell later said that Tecumseh "was a man of great courage and conduct" who was often found running into battle ahead of more experienced warriors.

It was in this raid that Tecumseh's compassion toward prisoners was established. According to Shawnee tradition, Tecumseh should only stand and watch if a captor decided to torture a prisoner (now considered the captor's property) to death. But not even tribal tradition could prevent Tecumseh from speaking out. He was a young man and new to the warrior's path, so it took great courage to do so—but speak out he did. Ruddell said Tecumseh "expressed great abhorrence" over a particularly brutal killing of one captive. Tecumseh's speech and arguments were so powerful and moving that "finally it was concluded among them not to [torture and kill] any more prisoners that should afterwards be taken."

Indian torture of prisoners was often extraordinarily brutal. The white prisoner in this 1886 wood engraving is quite lucky because instead of being burned or cut to pieces, he is simply tied to stakes in the ground as his captor watches him.

It was not long after this raid that Cheeseekau made an important decision for the family: They would go west. At that time, the land west of the Mississippi River belonged to Spain.

Stephen Ruddell (1768–1845)

As a young man raised by the Shawnee, Stephen Ruddell fought against other white men in a number of Indian battles. If he had been captured by the whites during this period, he would have been killed outright as a traitor to his race. Years later, after becoming an adult, Ruddell returned to white society. He kept his life with the Shawnee quiet or downplayed his role as a Shawnee warrior. He eventually became a Baptist preacher and was successful in converting his old Shawnee friends. Near the end of his life, he did open up a little, but by all accounts he was still very discreet about his life with the Shawnee. Ruddell died in 1845 and was described by his son as "a Natural orator, a man of great firmness & unbounded benevolence, an affectionate Husband & kind Father, an exemplary Christian."

The capture and raising of white children by Indians continued into the late 19th century. This 1886 photograph is of a young white boy who, like Stephen Ruddell, had become a member of the tribe that captured him, in this case the Apache band led by the famous leader Geronimo.

A French Canadian, Louis Lorimer, had arranged with the local Spanish government to offer land to any Shawnee or Delaware Indians willing to settle there. The opportunity of a sanctuary under Spanish rule and protection was greeted with joy by many war-weary Indians in the Ohio River valley. Unlike British and American policies that created so much conflict in their lives, Spanish policy was more "live and let live." In the spring of 1788, at least six hundred Shawnee and Delaware families, including Tecumseh's, began the trek west.

Traveling to a False Refuge

At one point in their journey, the group Tecumseh was with came upon a herd of buffalo. Tecumseh and other hunters immediately mounted their horses and galloped in pursuit. But shortly after the chase had begun, Tecumseh's horse threw him

The habitat of the American bison, commonly referred to as buffalo, was mostly in the Great Plains, though they once ranged as far east as the Appalachian Mountains. This 19th-century Currier & Ives print depicts a typical buffalo hunt in the Great Plains.

and Tecumseh fell onto the ground so hard that one of his thighbones shattered.

The group's migration west had to stop until Tecumseh could travel. Near the junction of the Tennessee and Ohio rivers, the Indians established a camp where they lived over the winter while Tecumseh's leg healed. The following spring, Tecumseh was healthy enough to travel. But from that point on, Tecumseh walked with a limp.

Cheeseekau's group finally reached the territory of Missouri in 1789 and was granted a parcel of land by the Spanish. Not long afterward, however, Americans led by George Morgan, a businessman that bought and sold frontier land to colonists, arrived to establish an American colony at New Madrid in Missouri. Though Morgan assured the Shawnee and Delaware Indians that these colonists would respect their rights and preserve the peace, trouble erupted.

Cheeseekau decided that instead of relying on other whites to protect them from Americans, he would ally himself and his family with other Indians. Thus he and his Shawnee group soon left, this time traveling southeast to the land of the Chickamauga Cherokee—at the time the fiercest and strongest enemies of the Long Knives. When they arrived at Lookout Mountain near present-day Chattanooga, Tennessee, they received a warm welcome. Tecumseh remained among the Cherokee for the next two years, gaining their respect as a warrior and hunter. By the time he decided to return to Ohio, he had risen to the level of a minor war chief and was clearly on the path of tribal leadership.

Tecumseh remained among the Cherokee for the next two years, gaining their respect as a warrior and hunter.

This photograph of the Tennessee River is taken from the summit of Lookout Mountain, where Tecumseh was welcomed by the Cherokee Indians.

While Tecumseh was earning his reputation, Cheeseekau was developing one as well. By 1792, Cheeseekau, whom the white men also called Shawnee Warrior, had become a great war chief and was feared by all whites in the Tennessee region. Once again, efforts to form an Indian confederacy to block American settlements was being attempted. This time the advocates were even more ambitious. They sought to create an alliance that would stretch from the Gulf Coast north to the Great Lakes. Cheeseekau was one of the many chiefs calling for this confederacy.

But in September Cheeseekau was killed in an incident known as the Battle of Buchanan's Station. The confederacy lost an important member. And Tecumseh lost a brother whom he loved and admired.

CHAPTER 4

Fall of the Pan-Tribal Confederacy

[Tecumseh] drove the artillery men from their posts, cut loose the horses, mounted them and [victoriously rode away].

—Stephen Ruddell, describing Tecumseh at the Battle of Fallen Timbers

In 1792, Shawnee chiefs sent out a summons for an intertribal conference. Tribal representatives from as far south as Alabama and as far north as the Saint Lawrence River in eastern Canada came to attend the conference. In October, they gathered at the junction of the Maumee and Auglaize rivers in northwest Ohio, where the city of Defiance now stands. It was an impressive gathering. Almost two dozen tribes were represented. Many speeches of Indian unity were made, along with promises to protect and defend tribal lands from white settlement.

A **wampum** belt symbolizing the confederacy was made. The war chiefs

Wampum belts constructed out of beads made from the shell of a sea snail were highly prized by many Native American cultures. The belts were used as money and to signify important events. This elaborate Iroquois wampum belt was probably created for a very special ceremony.

Tribal Councils

Tribal councils were called whenever an event or situation that affected the future of the tribe as a whole occurred. Messengers carrying wampum belts that signified a summons to council would visit the different villages. Sometimes villages sent representatives, such as their chiefs. Other times entire villages attended the tribal council. Once the tribe had gathered, the top chiefs of the nation would officially state the reason or reasons for the council and present possible solutions. Then the debates began. Because everyone had an equal voice in a council, anyone could discuss the issue, though usually the debates were handled by village chiefs. Once the debates concluded, the matter was put to a vote. Only if there was an overwhelming majority for or against an issue was it considered settled. Problems occurred when no decision was reached because this meant that the individual divisions, sometimes even individual villages, could make their own decision, which could be in conflict with other members of the tribe.

This 19th-century engraving shows the Ottawa chief Pontiac in council. He is probably holding a wampum belt in his left hand.

who would lead the tribes into battle included Blue Jacket, regarded as the Shawnee's greatest war chief, who also had the reputation as the greatest warrior among all the gathered tribes.

A Weak Confederacy

Despite all the fine words and ceremonies expressing solidarity, the confederacy's strength and unity was unreliable. Traditional rivalries and hatred between tribes continued, and even the threat of more white settlements could not entirely overcome this tribal self-interest. There were practical hurdles as well. Some tribes, such as the Seneca, lived close to large white settlements and would be among the first Indians to suffer retaliation. Others, such as the Iroquois in Canada and the Chickamauga in Alabama and Tennessee, were too far away to offer much more than moral support.

In actuality, the strength of the confederacy lay with the tribes living along the Maumee and Auglaize rivers who could supply about two thousand warriors. Yet for those warriors to be effective against the well-armed American militias, they would need modern firearms as well. That meant support from their old colonial master, the British.

But the British were in a delicate position. They were involved in a war with the new revolutionary government in France. The last thing the British government wanted was an outbreak of a new war in North America because the British could not afford to fight two wars at the same time. Yet they wanted to maintain influence with the Indians. The British government decided to give some guns,

Despite all the fine words and ceremonies expressing solidarity, the confederacy's strength and unity was unreliable.

ammunition, and supplies to the confederacy. Parliament hoped that the help was not enough to anger the Americans and give them an excuse to declare war against Britain.

Redcoat Promises

As the Shawnee prepared for battle, they received news that gave them encouragement. The new territorial governor of Canada, Lord Dorchester (also known as Sir Guy Carleton), was convinced that within a year, the United States would ally itself with France and declare war against Great Britain. Because many Americans had publicly demanded that their country invade and conquer Canada, he believed that soon the American government would try to do so. As he saw it, the best way to protect Canada was to strengthen his alliance with the Indians. In violation of the peace treaty Britain had signed with the United States, Lord Dorchester ordered a British outpost, Fort Miami, to be constructed in northern Ohio Territory, along the banks of the Maumee River. This fort would be **garrisoned** with British army troops. It would serve the dual

Guy Carleton, 1st Baron Dorchester, was a British general during the American Revolution. He successfully defended Lower Canada from invasion by American troops during the early years of that war.

purpose of an outpost guarding Canada and a refuge for Indians fighting against the Americans.

The Shawnee soon received more exciting news. The British lieutenant governor of Upper Canada, John Graves Simcoe, told the Indians that Britain would soon go to war against the United

States and reclaim the Ohio region. Simcoe had exaggerated, but the Shawnee were now convinced that their confederacy had the full support of the British. All they had to do was stop the American army—called the Legion of the United States—that was marching through Ohio. The army had been organized and trained by the Revolutionary War hero Major General "Mad" Anthony Wayne.

Wayne began his campaign by building a series of forts to secure his supply and communications lines. By 1794, his most recent, Fort Recovery, was only sixty miles from the large Indian camp on the Glaize River. General Wayne and his army were at Fort Greenville just east of what is today the border between

Major General Anthony Wayne earned the nickname "Mad" Anthony during the American Revolution because he was such a bold commander that some subordinates thought he went crazy in battle.

Indiana and Ohio when Blue Jacket and the other war chiefs decided to strike.

The Campaign Begins

During the third week of June 1794, Tecumseh and his followers joined Blue Jacket's allied Indian army, which totaled almost twelve hundred warriors—large by Indian standards.

The original plan called for the main Indian army to drive south and cut General Wayne's lines of supply and communications. Once his army had been isolated, the warriors would surround Fort Greenville and attack. But trouble arose among the Indian leadership soon after their army began its advance. The Shawnee's allies of Ojibwa, Potawatomi, and Ottawa—known as the Three Fires—insisted that they should first attack Fort Recovery. Blue Jacket and the other Shawnee

Fort Recovery was one of a number of forts that General Wayne built during his campaign. The site was later made a historic landmark, and a replica of the original fort, seen in this photograph, was built.

chiefs disagreed. They regarded the attack on Fort Recovery as a sideshow. Even if it were successful, the victory would not seriously hurt Wayne's army. But the Three Fires were important allies of the confederacy, so the Shawnee were forced to accept this change.

At dawn on June 30, Tecumseh was among the large group of warriors that attacked the fort. At first the battle went well for them. They ambushed a supply train, captured more than two hundred pack animals, and killed or scattered the guards and food providers. But things took a turn for the worse when they assaulted the fort itself. Fort Recovery had a larger garrison than they expected—more than one hundred soldiers under the command of Captain Alexander Gibson. Two frontal assaults by the Three Fires warriors were fought off with heavy losses among the Indians. The warriors backed down and a

At dawn on June 30, Tecumseh was among the large group of warriors that attacked the fort.

siege commenced that lasted for the rest of the day. That evening, even after Shawnee reinforcements arrived, the Three Fires chiefs decided to call off the attack.

Angry over their inability to capture the fort, the Three Fires chiefs blamed their failure on the Shawnee—claiming that reinforcements arrived too late to be of any use. As a result, the Three Fires chiefs announced that they and their warriors were leaving the Indian army and returning to their villages.

The departure of this large group of allies weakened the army to the point that Blue Jacket realized he was not strong enough to fight General Wayne and his troops. The confederacy's campaign was over before it could begin.

Action at Fallen Timbers

When General Wayne received news of what had occurred, he seized the initiative. His army, about thirty-five hundred men strong, included about fifteen hundred Kentucky volunteers. They quickly advanced north, taking the unprepared Indians by surprise. Indian villages in the army's path were hastily abandoned. Blue Jacket and his main ally, Delaware chief Buckongahelass, were able to assemble about fifteen hundred warriors to stop Wayne. Among that group were Tecumseh and his band.

In earlier frontier battles, the American troops were more often than not poorly trained and led. This caused them to panic

In this undated illustration, Major General "Mad" Anthony Wayne (center) is accompanied by members of his army, the Legion of the United States. His training of the Legion would prove decisive in the Battle of Fallen Timbers.

when ambushed by Indians screaming blood-curdling war cries. But General Wayne had spent months disciplining and training his troops. He was ready for whatever confrontation was about to occur with the Indians.

During the week of August 15, Buckongahelass and Blue Jacket took up defensive positions along the Maumee River, four miles south of the British outpost of Fort Miami. The location favored the defenders. Their left flank was anchored by the river, their right flank by a high bluff that was heavily forested. A recent storm had passed through the region, felling a number of trees. This gave the warriors stationed in the river valley natural, if haphazard, defense walls and barriers. The river valley was covered with tall grass that provided excellent cover for ambush. Finally, with the British fort at their rear, they had a ready source of ammunition and supplies. The fort would also provide a promised refuge in case they were forced to retreat.

Tecumseh and his band, reinforced by another group of warriors, were hidden in the tall grass bordering the northwestern bank of the river. As luck would have it, this group would have the honor of firing the first shots. On the morning of August 20, Tecumseh saw the approaching mounted advance guard made up of Kentucky militiamen under the command of Major William Price. The young warrior prepared his ambush, but what he didn't know was that instead of the anticipated fifteen hundred or so warriors behind him, there were only about five hundred in place to oppose the Legion of the United States. The rest of the warriors were either at Fort Miami, drawing supplies, or en route from their villages.

As soon as Major Price's **cavalry** were in range, Tecumseh and his warriors rose out of the grass and fired a round of shots.

At Fallen Timbers, Tecumseh encountered Kentucky militiamen—civilians that were recruited to aid the regular army. This photograph shows a group of frontier militia reenactors and a replica of a frontier fort.

They then ducked back down, reloaded, and less than a minute later fired a second round. Six soldiers fell, dead. The Kentucky militiamen had not had the discipline training of Wayne's military troops. Panicking, the surviving soldiers turned around and galloped away in retreat. Tecumseh's warriors, shouting their war cries, immediately began their pursuit—and ran headlong into part of the main body of General Wayne's army, who held their ground. Cavalry and **infantry** in coordinated counter attacks advanced along the entire Indian defensive line. Though outgunned and outnumbered, the Indians refused to panic. They fell back in good order.

This 19th-century engraving depicts a scene from the Battle of Fallen Timbers, which ended in an American victory over the Shawnee and their allies.

British Betrayal

Tecumseh stubbornly held his position, rallying his warriors and dangerously exposing himself to enemy fire. Then, seeing that he was about to be surrounded, he signaled for his warriors to retreat.

Blue Jacket and the other chiefs knew that once they gained refuge behind the **palisades** of Fort Miami, they could still win. But when the warriors reached the fort, they discovered its gates closed and locked. A number of warriors pounded on the wooden entrance and walls and called out to the British soldiers, demanding to be let in.

But the fort's commander, Major William Campbell, was afraid that if he allowed the warriors inside, his action would give the United States an excuse to declare war against Great Britain. He ordered that the gates remain closed. Looking out at the hundreds of warriors, he shouted, "I cannot let you in!"

The most shameful act in the Battle of Fallen Timbers was the British refusal to let the warriors into Fort Miami. Hal Sherman's illustration shows Blue Jacket calling for the British to open the gates. Never again would Tecumseh ever completely trust British promises of support.

The Indians were furious. But with General Wayne's army closing fast, they could not remain. Together with their women, children, and elderly members who had temporarily camped near the fort, they left. The group went north to the Indian base at Swan Creek, where Toledo is now located.

General Wayne was content to let the Indians go unharmed to Swan Creek. He felt his campaign had done enough damage to the Indians' cause. He turned his army around and returned to Fort Defiance in northwest Ohio Territory.

During the winter of 1794–1795, tribes began to abandon the confederacy. Before he lost too much power, in February 1795, Blue Jacket negotiated an **armistice** with the American commissioners. A formal peace treaty would be negotiated that summer.

"Mad" Anthony Wayne (1745–1796)

Anthony Wayne was a successful farmer and tanner in Pennsylvania when the American Revolution began. He became one of General George Washington's most respected generals during the war. His most famous battle was the capture of the British-held fort at Stony Point in 1779, where he got the nickname "Mad" Anthony because of how he conducted himself during the heat of battle. At the end of the war, the government gave him a large grant of land in Georgia, where he settled. When war broke out in the West, President George Washington recalled him to military service. He successfully ended the Northwest Indian War and negotiated the Treaty of Greenville, which ended the conflict. Wayne died of illness during a trip to Pennsylvania, and his body was buried in what is now Erie, Pennsylvania. Wayne's family wished for him to be buried in the family cemetery in Radnor, Pennsylvania. The general's body was removed from his grave and then packed into the back of a wagon for the trip to Radnor. For reasons unknown, a number of his bones were lost during the trip. As a result, legend has it that his ghost wanders the highway between the two cities, searching for those lost bones.

The Battle of Stony Point was one of General Wayne's greatest victories. This 19th-century wood engraving shows General Wayne directing an attack against British positions.

CHAPTER 5

Rise of a New Chief

I am alone the acknowledged head of all the Indians.

Following their defeat at the Battle of Fallen Timbers, Blue Jacket together with chiefs from tribes of the now-disbanded confederacy prepared to meet General Wayne at Fort Greenville. Tecumseh received a message about the meeting but chose to ignore it. He had no intention of adding his name to a document that he hated. His father and two older brothers had died fighting the whites. With the confederacy, he had seen what was possible when the different tribes banded together. He was already thinking of how he could form a new pan-tribal confederacy to stop the U.S. military forces.

The Treaty of Greenville

That summer, Chiefs Blue Jacket, Red Pole, and Black Hoof of the Shawnee as well as chiefs from the Wyandot, Delaware, Ottawa, Chippewa, Potawatomi, Miami, Wea, Kickapoo, and Kaskaskia tribes signed their marks to the Treaty of Greenville.

The tribes pledged to remain at peace and return all prisoners captured during the recent war. In addition, they agreed to surrender all tribal claims to eastern, central, and southern Ohio. A boundary known as the Greenville Treaty Line was established to separate Indian lands and white settlement in what the American government called the

An Indian chief presents a wampum belt to the U.S. delegates in this Howard Chandler Christy painting *Signing the Treaty of Greene Ville*. Tecumseh was one of the few influential chiefs who refused to attend the signing.

Northwest Territory. The federal government promised to enforce the boundary.

The federal government also gave the Indians trade goods of blankets, utensils, tools, livestock, and other items having a total value of $20,000 (about $340,000 in today's money). The government also agreed to make annual payments forever to the individual tribes in amounts that ranged from $500 (about $8,500 today) to $1,000 (about $17,000).

The Shawnee chiefs knew that by signing this treaty they were not only giving up land, but they were also taking a major step in abandoning their traditional way of life and adapting to white culture. They didn't like signing the treaty, but they believed that it was the only thing they could do. If they didn't sign, they

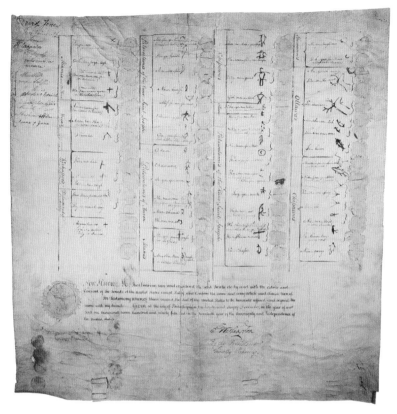

This is the last signature page of the Treaty of Greenville. There were so many Native American chiefs and U.S. delegates in attendance that it took two pages to record all their signatures.

knew the Americans would still take their land, and they'd get nothing in return.

Growing Respect and Influence

Now in his mid-twenties, Tecumseh was approaching the prime of his life. He stood five feet ten inches tall, making him above average in height. He was also in excellent physical

The Northwest Territory

The official name for the region was "the Territory Northwest of the River Ohio." Also known as the Old Northwest, it was the first national territory of the United States. The region included what are now the states of Ohio, Indiana, Illinois, Michigan, Wisconsin, and part of Minnesota.

Until the 1740s, the Northwest Territory was populated exclusively by Native American tribes. Contact with white men was limited to explorers or traders. Great Britain ceded the area to the United States in the Treaty of Paris, which ended the American Revolution. Hostilities between local tribes and American troops and settlers were frequent, and a number of wars were fought. By the 1840s, the tribes had lost most of their land in this region, and many were forced to migrate to **reservations** far from their ancestral homelands.

A map of the American frontier shows in pink "the Territory Northwest of the River Ohio," as the Northwest Territory was officially called.

condition. He had earned the respect and admiration of his people through his courage as a warrior and his compassion and generosity as a leader. He had also honed his skills as a speaker, and among a people who admired great oratory, Tecumseh "was naturally eloquent, very fluent, graceful in his gesticulation, but not in the habit of using very many gestures. There was no violence, no vehemence in his mode of delivering his speeches. He always made a great impression on his audience."

In addition to these much-admired qualities, Tecumseh was a very skilled hunter. A story is told how, one day, some of his fellow warriors came to him with a challenge. They bet that they could kill as many deer as he over a three-day period. Tecumseh accepted the bet. Three days later the tally was made. Tecumseh had brought into camp thirty deer—more than double his nearest competitor, who had bagged only twelve.

Because wild animals were the primary source of meat for Native Americans, warriors who were also good hunters were highly respected. This c. 1908 photograph shows a Sioux warrior stalking a buck.

Recognizing Tecumseh's growing influence, Blue Jacket visited Tecumseh on his way back from Fort Greenville and explained to him the details of the treaty in the hope that he would sign it. But Tecumseh again refused. He knew that signing the treaty would be betraying what his father and brother had stood for.

Tecumseh was so focused on the duties of chieftainship and the way of the warrior that it appears he had little time for personal relationships. He did not marry until 1796, but the marriage did not last. Shawnee custom made divorces easy, and the two soon parted. He married again—this time to a Shawnee woman named Mamate, who was a little older than him. According to villagers, the marriage was done "more in compliance with the wishes of others" than for love. They had one son, Pachetha, born possibly in 1800. Mamate died shortly after the boy's birth. The upbringing of Tecumseh's son was passed to his sister, Tecumapese.

Tecumseh was so focused on the duties of chieftainship and the way of the warrior that it appears he had little time for personal relationships.

The time was nearing when Tecumseh would take the next step and become a great chief. As such, he would build a new pan-tribal confederacy that would keep white settlers from overrunning their land. There was much to be done, and he would receive help from an unexpected source—someone who was almost an outcast of the tribe: his younger brother, Lalawethika.

The Shawnee Prophet

Lalawethika, born seven years after Tecumseh, was the black sheep of the family. In fact, everything that Tecumseh was, his brother was the opposite. Lalawethika had been a chubby, ill-tempered child who showed no skill in hunting and even less interest in the way of the warrior. Because he had lost an eye in a hunting accident as a boy, he was also disfigured. Lalawethika attempted to mask his failings through boasting, which only further alienated him from members of the village. With a taste for trader rum, Lalawethika was an alcoholic. He frequently got into arguments and beat his wife and children.

Though Tecumseh went out of his way to help his younger brother, there were times when he became quite angry with Lalawethika. This undated hand-colored engraving depicts a furious Tecumseh pulling Lalawethika's hair.

Only Tecumseh went out of his way to care for Lalawethika, who then tried to become a medicine man. But villagers did not trust him. When Lalawethika could not stop the ravages of an epidemic that killed several villagers in early 1805, it seemed that he was doomed to a life of failure.

That future changed one night in November 1805. Lalawethika was in the process of lighting his pipe when suddenly he collapsed. He was in such a deep coma that neither his wife nor his neighbors could detect any sign of life.

Then, amazingly, Lalawethika awoke. Astonished neighbors crowded into his wigwam to both see him and hear his astonishing tale of death, resurrection, and deliverance. He said he had visited heaven—a place without white men. He said the Shawnee had to reject the whites' ways or their souls would suffer a terrible fate in the afterlife.

At the conclusion of his tale, Lalawethika began trembling and crying. He then renounced his evil ways and said that he would never again touch the white man's alcohol. He also renounced the name of Lalawethika, and took for himself a new name: Tenskwatawa, "the Open Door." It was a name that symbolized his new life as a

This 1836 color lithograph of Tenskwatawa, the Prophet, shows him wearing a turbanlike cap, which was typical Shawnee headdress at that time. His right eye had been disfigured in a hunting accident.

holy man and **prophet** who would lead his people to paradise. Because of his prophecies, he also came to be known as the Shawnee Prophet.

Visions for a New Pan-Tribal Confederacy

Some Shawnee were skeptical, but Tecumseh saw that his brother's new religion could be useful to his own plans, and he supported his brother. Over the next few weeks, Tenskwatawa had additional visions that offered more details about how the Shawnee should live their lives. To the Shawnee and other tribes that had suffered at the hands of the Long Knives, Tenskwatawa's message was a powerful one. His new religion swept through the region like wildfire, gathering converts. By the summer of 1806, Tenskwatawa had so many followers that he had to establish a new village in the western Ohio Territory that came to be called Prophetstown.

The village of Prophetstown attracted many Native Americans in the Northwest Territory. This photograph is a model of what the village probably looked like and shows both homes and council buildings.

As this revival grew, Tecumseh saw an opportunity to finally realize his vision of a new pan-tribal confederacy. The main purpose of his confederacy was to keep Indian land out of the hands of the American government and its citizens. One of the definitions for *pan* is "all," so his "pan-tribal confederacy" could also be called an "all-tribe confederacy." As he envisioned it, the confederacy member tribes would keep their individual rights as a tribe, but would collectively share in the ownership of all Indian land in the confederacy regardless of where they actually lived. He insisted that the only way any land could be sold would be if *all* the members of the confederacy agreed to sell. Because tribal politics could be fragmented into small special interests, the insistence on an agreement by all the tribes would make such a sale pretty much impossible. Unfortunately, Tecumseh had to overcome that fragmentation in order to achieve his goal. That was not going to be easy.

CHAPTER 6

Growing Tensions

I mean to bring all tribes together.

The rapid growth of the Prophet's following began to concern Indiana Territory governor William Henry Harrison. If the Prophet's movement became larger, it could turn into a threat to the United States. In an attempt to reduce the Prophet's popularity, Harrison denounced him as a "pretended prophet" and an "imposter." Then, Harrison called on the Delaware tribe to challenge the Prophet's claim of being a messenger of the Great Spirit: "If he is really a prophet, ask of him to cause the sun to stand still— the moon to alter its course—the rivers to cease to flow—or the dead to rise from their graves. If he does these things, you may then believe that he has been sent from God."

The Prophecy

During the spring of 1806, astronomers had been establishing observation stations in Kentucky, Indiana, and Illinois to study the eclipse of the sun that was scheduled to occur on June 16. Perhaps Harrison knew of their work and either forgot or dismissed it as unimportant for the Indians. If so, he made a major miscalculation. Somehow, the Prophet became aware of the impending eclipse and

Then, Harrison called on the Delaware tribe to challenge the Prophet's claim of being a messenger of the Great Spirit . . .

saw in Harrison's challenge an opportunity to boost his reputation among the Indians.

Among the Shawnee, the eclipse was called *Mukutaaweethee Keesohtoa*, a "Black Sun." It was an event that filled the Shawnee with dread, since they believed it was an omen that warned of war. It is not clear how Tenskwatawa found out about the eclipse, but there is some speculation that suggests it was Tecumseh who had learned of the eclipse—possibly through some people he might have known who had read about it in an **almanac**.

In early June, the Prophet assembled a number of his followers at Greenville and boldly announced that he would soon use his power as a messenger of the Master of Life, or Great Spirit, to darken the sun at midday. He instructed them to travel to as many villages as they could and spread the word of the miracle that he would perform on June 16.

His announcement startled his followers, who hastened to obey him. On the morning of June 16, a large number of Indians from nearby tribes gathered around the Prophet's hut. The Prophet added to the tension by remaining inside the hut all morning. At noon, when daylight began to turn into

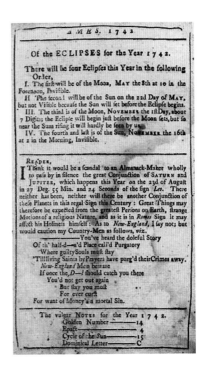

It was thought that the Prophet used an almanac to predict an eclipse. Farmers relied heavily on information provided in an almanac for planting and harvesting their crops. This page from a 1742 almanac states the days and times of eclipses for that year.

A solar eclipse occurs when the moon passes between Earth and the sun. This NASA photograph shows an eclipse almost at its high point, when the moon is centered over the sun.

eerie twilight, the Prophet stepped out of his hut. Staring at the frightened crowd, he shouted, "Did I not speak the truth? See, the sun is dark!"

Noting the terror in the group, he then stated that just as he had darkened the sun, he would now restore its light. Within seconds, daylight returned. The Indians were not only relieved, they were also convinced that the Prophet truly was a messenger of the Master of Life. As the Prophet expected, news of the miracle caused his reputation to soar, and more and more converts flocked to Greenville.

A Bully of a Governor

William Henry Harrison had become governor of Indiana Territory when he was just twenty-seven years old. Tall, handsome, and ambitious, he was determined to obtain as much Indian land as he could for the United States.

In 1802, two years after becoming governor, he began his land grab. Over the course of three years, he signed seven treaties with eleven tribes that transferred to the United States what is now southern Indiana, most of Illinois, and parts of Wisconsin and Missouri for the unjust bargain price of two cents an acre or less (about thirty-nine cents today).

Harrison used every negotiating trick in the book to get his way. He bribed important Indian leaders, and he threatened to block payments and supplies guaranteed by earlier treaties. He got Indian leaders drunk before he began negotiating, he exploited the poverty of weak tribes, and he used tribal rivalries to isolate reluctant tribes. In the rare instance when a tribe still refused to sell its land, Harrison would resort to fraud. He would visit a neighboring tribe and buy the land from it, even though that tribe had no hereditary claim to the land he wanted to buy. As soon as he had a signed document, Harrison turned around and kicked the real owners off their land.

William Henry Harrison, shown here in a mid-19th-century Currier & Ives lithograph portrait, used his influence as governor of the Indiana Territory to grab as much Indian land as possible.

As white farmers settled on Native American land, they cut down trees and depleted resources that were essential for the survival of the Indians. Rivers and lakes became the "highways" of the frontier, as this 19th-century wood engraving of a Virginia settlement in the 1700s shows.

Most of the time, Indian leaders had no choice but to sell. It was getting harder for tribes to live off the land as their ancestors did. Game and furs from animals were becoming increasingly scarce because more and more forests were being cut down and turned into farmland for the growing number of white settlers. This situation forced tribes to become increasingly dependent on the federal government for their livelihood. The only way the Indian leaders could guarantee that help was to sell large parts of their homeland. It was an emotional decision made worse because it exposed the helplessness of Indian leaders to care for the future of their people.

Building New Pan-Tribal Unity

Some chiefs, seeing the growing power of the United States, decided that their future lay in agreeing to compromise. But a growing number of Native Americans hated the idea of abandoning their traditional way of life in favor of living as the whites did.

Tecumseh saw these clashing opinions as an opportunity, and he took it. Through personal visits and his representatives, he delivered a message to different villages that was both simple and clear: Indians must set aside their tribal differences and interests and stand together as one communal group—a pan-tribal confederacy—to save their lands, their cultures, and their independence. They were reminded that such confederacies had happened before during other times of crisis. He emphasized the concept that the land was the common property of *all* the tribes and its defense was a shared responsibility. Using a metaphor that the Indians would understand, he called the land a large cooking pot and each tribe a serving spoon.

Even while Tecumseh continued his campaign for a new pan-tribal confederacy, tension between the Indians and the United States continued, and by 1809, it had increased to a point at which it seemed war could break out any day. White settlers remained deeply suspicious of the Prophet and his movement, and they blamed him for every hostile action committed by Indians. The Prophet managed to convince territorial leaders, including Harrison, that he and his followers were not to blame, which was true. The attacks were made by individual warriors, often from other tribes, acting on their own.

> *He emphasized the concept that the land was the common property of* all *the tribes and its defense was a shared responsibility.*

Meeting With the Redcoats

For his part, Tecumseh, together with a number of other chiefs, traveled across the Saint Clair River from Fort Detroit (in present-day Michigan) and headed toward the town of Amherstburg in Canada. They planned to have a council with the British lieutenant governor of Upper Canada, Francis Gore, to see what sort of assistance they could get from their former ally.

Gore was sympathetic, but like previous British officials, he was in a delicate position. The British government had few troops in Canada and, because of the war in Europe, could not send more. Gore spoke at length of British friendship with the Indians. Though he was careful to avoid talk of going to war, he made it clear that if the Shawnee and other tribes chose to do so, the British would help. This assistance would be in the form of supplying weapons and ammunition. Most importantly, if the tribes won, the British would help them overturn the recent treaties that gave the United States much of Ohio. At the end of the council, Gore presented a beautiful wampum belt that symbolized the British-Indian alliance. The belt, edged in black, contained a large white band that ran the length of its center. In the white band was a heart flanked by figures representing Gore and the Indians.

Though the gift symbolizing solidarity pleased the chiefs, Tecumseh by now was experienced enough in the art of **diplomacy** to see that British help was limited. If Tecumseh and his allies chose the path of war with the United States, they would be on their own. Even so, when they departed, Tecumseh saw the council as a diplomatic triumph. The British territorial government now knew about him and his movement. Even though the offer of aid was limited, the offer had been made. That support gave him leverage both with his fellow Indians and with

Francis Gore was for the most part an effective administrator of Upper Canada. However, during his second term as lieutenant governor, he repeatedly clashed with the Canadian colonial legislature and resigned after serving just two years.

the United States, though he knew he would have to be careful in how he used it.

Treaty of Fort Wayne

Harrison was well aware of both the growing Indian discontent and the rising power of Tecumseh and the Prophet. Had he acted with sensitivity and restraint, he could have kept the Indians of the Old Northwest within the American camp, denying the British an important ally in North America. Unfortunately, he misinterpreted the facts and reached the erroneous conclusion that Tecumseh's and the Prophet's influence among Indians was

Fort Wayne, seen in this modern replica, was named after Major General "Mad" Anthony Wayne. Constructed near important trade routes in the region, a village rapidly grew around the original fort. Today, Fort Wayne is Indiana's second-largest city.

declining. This misunderstanding prompted him to try to buy more Indian land. In June 1809, he sent a message to chiefs of the Delaware, Eel River, Kickapoo, Miami, Potawatomi, and Wea tribes, summoning them to a council at Fort Wayne in September to discuss a new treaty.

A thousand Indians attended. Harrison made sure that most of them came from villages and tribes that were dependent on American aid. Harrison began the council with a speech to the group. His manner was polite, and the tone of his speech sounded reasonable and sincere. But his speech requesting the sale of yet another tract of land was packed with half-truths, distortions of facts, and outright lies. He said that the United States had always dealt fairly with the Indians, had fully lived up to its obligations in

William Henry Harrison (1773–1841)

William Henry Harrison was born on February 9, 1773, the son of a wealthy Virginia plantation owner who also signed the Declaration of Independence. He took part in a number of campaigns in the Old Northwest during the Northwest Indian War in the late 1700s. He left the army in 1798 and soon entered politics. He won election as a territorial delegate to Congress for the Northwest Territory and helped divide it into the territories of Ohio and Indiana. He was appointed the territorial governor of Indiana in 1800 and to a number of military commands. His battlefield successes made him a national hero.

As the Whig party candidate for president of the United States in 1840, Harrison's campaign slogan "Tippecanoe and Tyler Too" became one of the most famous political catchphrases of its time. It referred to Harrison's victory in the Battle of Tippecanoe and to his vice-presidential candidate, John Tyler. Harrison was inaugurated the ninth president of the United States at age sixty-eight. One month later, he contracted pneumonia and died. He was the first president to die in office, and his administration is the shortest of all the presidents.

Harrison's presidential campaign was one of the best-managed campaigns in American history. He capitalized on his victory at Tippecanoe by using the slogan "Tippecanoe and Tyler Too," as shown in this etching from his 1840 campaign.

past treaties, and had protected Indian rights against settlers. As for the disappearance of game, he blamed it on overhunting by Canadians and the Indians themselves. In separate meetings later, he played a divide-and-conquer game, manipulating already existing tribal rivalries and jealousies.

In the end, he got his way again. On September 30, 1809, the Treaty of Fort Wayne was signed. For a purchase price of only $5,250 (approximately $84,000 in today's money) in goods and some additional annual grants of money and supplies, Harrison had obtained three million acres of land, most in Indiana Territory, at an average price of less than two cents an acre.

The Question of Survival

When Tecumseh heard the news, he was furious. But he was smart enough to see that Harrison's greed could help his own cause. Tecumseh had repeatedly stated that the United States would not stop until it had bought all the Indians' land and had driven them away. The Treaty of Fort Wayne was the proof he needed. Tecumseh claimed the treaty was outright robbery. All the Indians in the region agreed. Not even the most pro-American chief was able to deny it.

The treaty spurred Tecumseh into greater action. By now, more than 270,000 white people had settled in the region. The combined population of the Indian tribes, on the other hand, numbered about seventy thousand. If things continued, there would soon be no Indians left. Faced with the threatening question of survival, Tecumseh now believed it was not a question of *if* he would go to war but *when*.

He began an intense campaign to unite the tribes. The following spring, in May 1810, Tecumseh pinned his hopes on an intertribal conference at Parc-aux-Vaches near the south end of the St. Joseph River along the Michigan and Indiana border. Tecumseh did not attend, and accounts suggest that his brother the Prophet delivered his arguments for him. Yet despite the facts and the Prophet's eloquence, the most important chiefs at the council still could not overcome their individual tribal interests and their jealousies of Tecumseh, his brother, and their movements. They rejected Tecumseh's calls for unity and war.

Faced with the threatening question of survival, Tecumseh now believed it was not a question of if he would go to war but when.

The furious outcry from the Indians following the signing of the Treaty of Fort Wayne caused Harrison to realize that he had gone too far and that the present crisis could lead to war. However, he refused to back down. In order to keep himself informed of Tecumseh and the Shawnee Prophet's actions, he sent agents and friendly chiefs to the Parc-aux-Vaches council. When they told him that Tecumseh's proposals had been defeated, Harrison believed that the worst of the crisis had passed and that he still held the upper hand. Believing that he was now in a position of strength, he decided to make a show of being kind and generous.

CHAPTER 7

A Fateful Meeting

Sell a country! Why not sell the air, the clouds, and the Great Sea, as well as the earth?

At this point, Harrison believed that the Prophet had greater influence than Tecumseh and that the younger Shawnee brother was his main opponent. Harrison therefore chose to send a message to the Prophet, stating that though he regarded the Prophet as an enemy of the United States, the chain of friendship between the two was not beyond repair.

Aware of Tecumseh's diplomatic efforts with the British at Amherstburg, Harrison also wrote: "I know your warriors are brave. Ours are not less so, but what can a few brave warriors do against the innumerable warriors of the Seventeen Fires [United States]." He cautioned Tecumseh against counting on British help and protection. Harrison wrote that if war broke out between the United States and Great Britain, the United States would win and seize Canada.

Though Harrison had no intention of surrendering any land purchased in the Treaty of Fort Wayne, he concluded his message by writing that he would be willing to hear complaints about the treaty and that he had the power to restore land to its rightful owners if it had been wrongly sold. If the Prophet did not

[Harrison] cautioned Tecumseh against counting on British help and protection.

like that suggestion, Harrison added that he was free to travel to Washington, D.C., and present his case to the president. Harrison guaranteed safe passage for the Prophet and others that he might take with him. Harrison's offer to meet was accepted— by Tecumseh.

Making an Impression

Tecumseh arrived at Governor Harrison's home at Vincennes, Indiana Territory, with an entourage of about seventy-five warriors on August 12, 1810. Harrison and his group were sitting on a platform. When Harrison offered Tecumseh a seat beside him, Tecumseh replied, "[T]he earth was the most proper place for the Indians, as they liked to repose upon the bosom of their mother." Then he and his warriors sat down on the grass.

According to one chronicler, the effect of Tecumseh's reply was "electrical, and for some moments there was a perfect

During the few meetings between Harrison and Tecumseh, each was so suspicious of the other that, as this hand-colored illustration of their meeting at Vincennes shows, the possibility of violence always existed.

silence." For a brief instant, Harrison did not know what to say. In the past he had always been able to intimidate chiefs, even powerful ones. Using tactics that had worked in the past, he began by telling Tecumseh that he promised to listen fairly to the chief's claims. Harrison insisted that he had always treated the Indians fairly and justly and that Tecumseh was the first and only chief to accuse him of dishonorable dealings. He blamed Tecumseh for stirring up hostility between the whites and the Indians with unfair statements about the sale of land in the Treaty of Fort Wayne. Finally, he challenged Tecumseh to say openly if it was true that he had made these statements.

Harrison had just made the biggest mistake imaginable, one that Tecumseh was prepared to seize with both hands. Tecumseh slowly rose to his feet and looked around at his audience. The atmosphere, already tense, became almost unbearable.

Tecumseh's Reply

Tecumseh looked at Harrison and the other white men. Then he began to speak, "Brother," he said, "I wish you to give me close attention, because I think you do not clearly understand. I want to speak to you about promises that the Americans have made."

Tecumseh then launched into a powerful speech that stunned the white men and electrified the Indians. Revealing a mastery of history, he listed the different treaties that had been signed, from the Treaty of Fort Finney in 1786 to the recent Treaty of Fort Wayne, and how the white men had broken the terms of earlier treaties. He also reminded them of the murder of Moluntha and that the officer who committed the brutal act had never been punished. He had to pause numerous times to allow interpreters to translate his words. After one such pause, he stared straight at

Harrison and said, "Brother, after such bitter events, can you blame me for placing little confidence in the promises of Americans?"

Then, because it seemed that American greed for Indian land would end only when the whites had taken *all* Indian land, Tecumseh said, "The only way to stop this evil is for all the [tribes] to unite in claiming an equal right in the land. That is how it was at first, and should be still, for the land never was divided, but was for the use of everyone. . . .

Tecumseh then launched into a powerful speech that stunned the white men and electrified the Indians.

"Sell a country! Why not sell the air, the clouds, and the Great Sea, as well as the earth? Did not the Great Spirit make them all for the use of his children?"

Tecumseh then demanded a return of land that he said was unfairly sold in the Treaty of Fort Wayne. To make absolutely sure that Harrison knew he was dealing with a chief who could not be bought or intimidated, he said, "I am Shawnee! I am a warrior! . . . I am the master of my own destiny! . . .

"Now, Brother, everything I have said to you is the truth. . . . I have declared myself freely to you about my intentions. . . . I want to know what you are going to do about taking our land. I want to hear you say that you understand now, and

Though tempers were frayed, despite the scene presented in this illustration, at no time during their meetings did Tecumseh actually threaten to kill Harrison on the spot.

you will wipe out that pretended treaty, so that the tribes can be at peace with each other, as you pretend you want them to be. Tell me, Brother. I want to know."

Harrison stared at Tecumseh in silence. Then he promised to give Tecumseh an answer soon. The situation was tense. A meeting followed later that day, but neither side would change its position. The council ended shortly after Harrison promised to forward Tecumseh's words to the president of the United States. Tecumseh and his followers soon departed. Both sides knew that they were enemies and that their differences could be settled only by war.

The fact that they were enemies did not lessen Harrison's respect for Tecumseh. Harrison wrote to Secretary of War William Eustis to explain the developing situation. In his letters, Harrison wrote that Tecumseh was "the great man of the [new Indian movement]."

William Eustis, shown above, was President James Madison's secretary of war from 1809–1813.

He also wrote, "If it were not for the vicinity of the United States, he [Tecumseh] would perhaps be the founder of an Empire that would rival . . . that of Mexico or Peru." Recalling the Shawnee chief's efforts to build his confederacy during the past four years, Harrison added, "[H]e has been in constant motion . . . [and] wherever he goes, he makes an impression favorable to his purposes."

But Harrison's respect for Tecumseh simply meant that he saw he had a powerful enemy who had to be defeated before becoming too strong to be destroyed.

CHAPTER 8

The Struggle for Power

[I will] wash away all these bad stories.

In the fall of 1810, American government representatives held two councils with the Indian tribes. The first was at Brownstown, Michigan Territory, and the second was at Fort Wayne, Indiana Territory. The purpose of these councils was to block Tecumseh's confederacy-building efforts. The government aimed to do this by getting the various chiefs to pledge peace and loyalty to the U.S. government and to reject any alliance with the British. Initially Tecumseh and his brother planned to attend the Brownstown council, but when they discovered that it would be dominated by pro-American chiefs, they decided not to attend.

Resentments and Jealousies

As the commissioners hoped, a number of the chiefs criticized Tecumseh and the Prophet. These chiefs, all much older and jealous of the two brothers' power and influence, regarded Tecumseh, in particular, as arrogant. They felt he unfairly claimed to be the acknowledged chief of all the Indians. They also verbally attacked the Prophet and his new religion. They bitterly claimed that the Prophet was causing their people to turn away from traditional chiefs and abandon ancient customs. They had no objection to the Prophet establishing Prophetstown and living apart from the other Indians—so long as he didn't try to gather more followers from their villages.

These statements against Tecumseh and the Prophet could not be wholly taken at face value. The brothers' movements had struck a nerve with all the chiefs who attended the two councils. However, even those chiefs who had become the U.S. Army's closest allies and had chosen to adapt to white culture were suspicious of the federal government and its future relations with their people. But their complaints were quieted by the lavish bribes of trade goods and an increase in the annual money payments.

> *The brothers' movements had struck a nerve with all the chiefs who attended the two councils.*

Although the U.S. government had the upper hand when it came to handing out food, goods, and money, the Prophet held the moral high ground and was not interested in keeping quiet. His speeches had successfully tapped into the long-standing resentment many young warriors had.

Supplies for War

Tecumseh, meanwhile, worked hard to obtain from the British the weapons he needed for the war that would inevitably occur between his confederacy and the Long Knives. His main contact was the trader Matthew Elliott, who was the ideal go-between. Elliott had lived for years among the Shawnee, and his wife was Shawnee. As a private individual, the British government was able to use him to maintain its relationship with the Indians and to encourage Indian resentment against the American government with little diplomatic risk to itself. If the American government got wind of Elliott's actions, the Canadian territorial government could accuse him of being a **renegade**. It was a claim that would be easily believed because each side had done this sort of thing for years.

Even as he was passing to Tecumseh the weapons and supplies the Shawnee chief needed, Elliott was advising Tecumseh to go slow. If Tecumseh's warriors attacked too soon, they'd be crushed by the Americans—and the British would do nothing to help. Recalling the memory of the locked gates at Fort Miami following the Battle of Fallen Timbers, Tecumseh heeded the advice. Though it was impossible for him to stop all of his impatient warriors from raiding white settlers, he did manage to keep their raids to a minimum.

Tecumseh . . . worked hard to obtain from the British the weapons he needed for the war that would inevitably occur between his confederacy and the Long Knives.

This period of relative peace proved brief. During the winter of 1810–1811, the number of Indian raids increased as hotheaded young warriors anxious to establish their reputations roamed the region. By the summer of 1811, both Tecumseh and the Prophet realized that war with the Long Knives would come sooner rather than later.

Matters seemed to come to a head in early July. Alarmed by the reports of increasing Indian hostilities, Indiana Territory governor William Henry Harrison wrote to Tecumseh and the Prophet and warned them to cease their activities and to remain in Prophetstown. If either attempted to leave, Harrison would send a large militia against them and destroy the village.

A Meeting Arranged

The warning was a clear challenge to Tecumseh and his new confederacy. The Shawnee chief knew that he did not have

Militia

The idea of a militia, in which civilians would temporarily band together and serve as soldiers during times of war to protect their families and property, began during colonial times in North America. The threat of Indian attacks on colonists was a constant danger, but stationing large groups of professional soldiers was expensive. Instead, European governments chose to station small groups of soldiers who would provide officers and train the colonists. When outbreaks of hostilities occurred, all able-bodied men who owned rifles were expected to join the militia in active service. The enlistment terms of this active duty were usually three to six months. The qualities of militias varied. A few were very good, but most were not. Many men saw the militia more as a social club than as a military organization. Discipline was often poor. Desertion rates were high. More often than not, militiamen ran away from battle in a panic before the first shot was fired. The organization of militias began to change in the early twentieth century with the formation of the National Guard.

This c. 1876 Currier & Ives lithograph depicts a local militia marching off to war during the American Revolution.

enough warriors to defeat Harrison's force. But if he bowed to Harrison's threat, he would lose respect among the Indian tribes. Tecumseh cunningly used the opportunity to turn the tables on Harrison. On July 4, 1811, he sent the territorial governor a message stating that Tecumseh himself would meet with Harrison in eighteen days "to wash away all these bad stories that have been circulated. When I come to Vincennes to see you, all will be settled in peace and happiness."

Tecumseh's message filled Harrison with alarm. He thought Tecumseh was stronger than he really was. He thought that this proposal of peace was actually a **Trojan-Horse trick**. He believed that once Tecumseh and his warriors greeted him and his aides, they'd attack. Harrison responded by telling Tecumseh that he could bring no more than thirty warriors.

When **scouts** that he had stationed along the banks of the Wabash River reported that Tecumseh was leading more than fifty canoes filled with warriors, Harrison was convinced that Tecumseh was planning to fight. He issued orders calling up federal troops and local militia. By late July, he had almost eight hundred armed men at his disposal. If Tecumseh wanted a fight, Harrison was prepared to give him one.

But a fight was the last thing Tecumseh wanted—at least, at that moment. The three hundred warriors in his party were there as a show of strength and for personal protection.

The term *Trojan Horse* refers to a form of trickery designed to defeat a foe. It is based on the ancient story of how the Greeks, hidden in a large wooden horse, entered the city of Troy and defeated it. This undated engraving shows the unsuspecting Trojans dragging the horse into their city.

What Harrison either forgot or ignored were the instances in the past when Shawnee and other chiefs had met army officers and other officials to negotiate peace in good faith, only to be murdered either by the officials themselves or by an out-of-control white mob.

Fears and Ill Will

With tensions near a breaking point, Tecumseh was not about to take any chances with his safety. At the same time, Tecumseh realized that his large group of warriors could send the wrong signal. Therefore, he included a second group that contained a significant number of women and children, because no war party ever traveled with their families.

Tecumseh and the first group of Indians arrived on July 27. Harrison wanted to immediately hold a council, but Tecumseh refused to be intimidated. He replied that the council would be held only after all his members arrived, which happened on July 30.

The council began with Tecumseh and his people on one side and Harrison supported by his armed troops on the other. Harrison began by forcefully making a number of complaints and demands. He acted as if he were deliberately trying to provoke Tecumseh into an attack. The governor demanded to know why the Prophet's followers had stolen a recent treaty-authorized shipment of salt that was meant for another band. Harrison also ordered Tecumseh to surrender the warriors who had recently staged raids against travelers and settlers. He finished by telling the

With tensions near a breaking point, Tecumseh was not about to take any chances with his safety.

Shawnee chief that he refused to discuss any return of Indian lands purchased through the Treaty of Fort Wayne.

Tecumseh replied by calmly telling Harrison that "the white people were unnecessarily alarmed" and that he and his brother wanted nothing but peace. As for Harrison's concerns about Tecumseh building an Indian confederacy, Tecumseh cunningly used the existence of Harrison's own nation as justification. The chief said, "The United States had set him the example of forming a strict union amongst all the fires [states] that compose their confederacy. The Indians did not complain of it—nor should his white brothers complain of him doing the same with regard to the Indian tribes."

Tecumseh also downplayed the problems regarding the seizure of the salt shipment, and dismissed the warrior raids by saying that they were not done by his or the Prophet's followers.

After five days, the council ended. Tecumseh told Harrison that he was taking twenty warriors with him and traveling south. Although he was planning on recruiting more Indian allies, he tried to give the impression that he was simply going to visit the Creek, to whom he was related through his mother. When he returned, he said, he'd be happy to meet with the president and settle everything.

If Tecumseh thought he had calmed Harrison's fears, he was wrong. Harrison still believed that the real reason Tecumseh had come to Vincennes was to kill him. The presence of so many warriors confirmed to Harrison that his suspicions were correct. As he saw it, the only reason that Tecumseh did not try was because Harrison had his own large bodyguard. Also, the council convinced Harrison that only swift military action would solve the growing Indian problem presented by Tecumseh and the Prophet.

Thus, instead of buying time, Tecumseh's action would cause the very thing he hoped to avoid. His decision to go south to gather more allies would eventually give Harrison the opening he needed to strike.

CHAPTER 9

The Journey South

I will stamp my foot on the ground and shake down every house in Tuckhabatchee.

Tecumseh arrived in the south at about the end of August. He planned to visit the Chickasaw, Choctaw, Creek, Seminole, and Cherokee nations. If he managed to convince them, then his confederacy—which already included members of the Potawatomi, Kickapoo, Winnebago, Shawnee, Miami, Wyandot, Wea, Piankeshaw, and other tribes in the North—would encircle the expanding United States from the Great Lakes to Florida.

This undated etching is believed to be a portrait of Tecumseh addressing a fellow chief. Tecumseh's efforts to convince chiefs to join his confederacy ultimately met with little success.

However, almost immediately his hopes turned into frustration. His meetings with the Chickasaw and Choctaw ended with them remaining neutral. Tecumseh refused to let their refusal discourage him. He believed he would have a more sympathetic audience with the next tribe he was going to meet: the Creek. They were a powerful tribe, and he was related to them through his mother. If he could get them on his side, that would go a long way toward convincing other tribes to join him.

A Timely Arrival

Tecumseh arrived at the important Creek village of Tuckhabatchee, in what is now Alabama, in late September. He picked the moment of his arrival well—during the annual council of the Creek confederacy. Fifteen different Creek tribes as well as members of the Chickasaw, Choctaw, and Cherokee nations were there. And because it was such an important council, a number of U.S. government agents also participated.

Tecumseh and his group arrived several days after the council had begun. They made a ceremonious entrance that electrified the crowd. One eyewitness later wrote, "Tecumseh, at the head of his . . . party, marched into the square. . . . They were entirely naked, except [for their breechcloths] and ornaments. Their faces were painted black, and their heads adorned with eagle plumes, while buffalo tails dragged from behind, suspended by bands which went around their waists. Buffalo tails were also attached to their arms, and made to stand out, by means of bands."

Tecumseh and his group . . . made a ceremonious entrance that electrified the crowd.

This impressive group marched around the village square a number of times before stopping in front of the group of

This portrait of Tecumseh is unusual because it shows him groomed and attired as if he were a white man. It is possible that the white artist added erroneous embellishments to the portrait.

assembled Creek chiefs. The chiefs were then presented with tobacco, the customary gesture of friendship.

Because federal agents were also at the council, Tecumseh refused to speak. What he had to say was for the ears of the Indians alone. Only after the agents had left, about a week later, did Tecumseh address the council. Tall and dressed in his best clothing, he had a commanding presence. Tecumseh looked over the crowd, letting the excitement in the audience build. Finally, he began to speak.

A Call to Unite

"*Brothers*," he said. "We all belong to one family; we are all children of the Great Spirit. We walk in the same path; slake [quench] our thirst at the same spring; and now affairs of the greatest concern lead us to smoke the pipe around the same council fire!"

He reminded them of the many things the Indians had done to help the first white settlers. Indians gave the whites food, helped them hunt, and gave them land to build their houses. Then he said, "*Brothers*—The white men are not friends to the Indians: At first they only asked for land sufficient for a wigwam; now, nothing will satisfy them but the whole of our hunting grounds, from the rising to the setting sun.

"*Brothers*—The white men want more than our hunting grounds; they wish to kill our warriors; they would even kill

This 1867 illustration, depicting the movement of the white settlers and railroads, confirms Tecumseh's statement regarding the white man's ever-growing hunger for Indian land. However, it does not fully present the brutal impact that displacement had on Native Americans.

our old men, women, and little ones."

Tecumseh spoke for hours. He reminded his audience of the many injustices the white men had committed on the Indians. He repeated how the American government had consistently turned a blind eye to them, leaving the Indians no choice but to seek justice on their own. He mixed the appeal of his brother's religious **fundamentalism** with his own call for pan-tribal unity. He claimed that they would be strong enough to resist the Long Knives and keep their independence. He finished his appeal by saying, "*Brothers*—We must be united; we must smoke the same pipe; we must fight each other's battles; and more than all, we must love the Great Spirit; he is for us; he will destroy our enemies, and make all his [tribes] happy."

Rejection

That Tecumseh was a great orator cannot be disputed. He spoke with passion and skill. Yet he failed to move his fellow "brothers" to action. Some of the assembled chiefs were too dependent on the federal agents and their annual gifts. Others felt threatened by the Prophet's religious fundamentalism. Still others were jealous of Tecumseh's popularity with the young warriors. Though none wished Tecumseh harm, neither would they reach out their hands in support.

Tecumseh made one last attempt. His mark was Big Warrior, the most influential of those chiefs that opposed or were neutral to the confederacy. Big Warrior was of mixed Creek and white blood. After he gave Big Warrior some gifts, Tecumseh made his appeal. When he finished, Big Warrior said he would not join Tecumseh's cause.

Tecumseh stood up. Looking down at Big Warrior, he said, "Your blood is white. . . . You have taken my talk and the [gifts] and the wampum and the hatchet, but you do not mean to fight. I know the reason. You do not believe the Great Spirit has sent me. You shall know." He then said he would leave Tuckhabatchee and go to Fort

An eloquent chief was capable of giving a speech that would last for hours. In this etching, Tecumseh is before a council of chiefs, delivering such a speech. Behind Tecumseh are some of his followers.

Detroit (present-day Detroit, Michigan). There, he would meet with tribes in the region as well as the British across the border in Canada. Once there, he told Big Warrior, "I will stamp my foot on the ground and shake down every house in Tuckhabatchee." Then Tecumseh turned away and left.

This seemingly angry statement would turn out to be the key to Tecumseh's change of luck.

CHAPTER 10

The Battle of Tippecanoe

*Governor Harrison made war on my people in
my absence.*

Tecumseh's journey south had begun in August and lasted
almost five months. Tecumseh sensed that Harrison
might try an attack while he was gone. Just before he left,
Tecumseh ordered his brother and the other chiefs at
Prophetstown to avoid at all costs any battle with the Long
Knives. But the population at Prophetstown contained a
large number of hotheaded young warriors who had no
appreciation or understanding of Tecumseh's long-term
plan. They wanted to attack the nearby vulnerable white
settlements now rather than later.

Just two months after Tecumseh had left for the south,
three young warriors raided a settlement and stole some
horses. This gave Harrison the excuse he needed. He would
wreck Tecumseh's power by attacking it at its base—
Prophetstown. The governor gathered his army and began
his march on the town, which was about 180 miles away.
Harrison's force contained about a thousand men. Roughly
a third of them were regular army soldiers. The rest was a
mixed group of militia and volunteers from Indiana
and Kentucky.

When the Prophet got word of Harrison's approach, he
tried to follow Tecumseh's instructions. But as Harrison's
army got closer, the Prophet became caught up in events
and found himself forced to fight.

Preparing for Battle

On October 1, Harrison halted his army at what is now Terre Haute, Indiana, and built Fort Harrison. This would be his advance base of operations for the attack on Prophetstown.

During the time of the army's advance, messengers from Prophetstown had traveled to nearby villages to request reinforcements. The response was enthusiastic; hundreds of warriors traveled to Prophetstown to help fight the Long Knives. Though the Prophet was not a warrior, his position as a spiritual leader made him an important individual in the days leading to the battle. The Prophet called upon the Master of Life and other spirits to help the warriors. He led the purification rituals and performed other necessary ceremonies to boost and sustain the morale of the warriors.

On November 6, 1811, scouts reported that Harrison's army was just one mile west of Prophetstown. Realizing that a fight in the open and in daylight would end in an Indian defeat, the

As seen in this undated etching, Fort Harrison was initially a small outpost. But the location had long been an important frontier trade stop, and by 1816, the town of Terre Haute was founded.

Prophet staged a ruse. He sent a small group of warriors under a white flag of truce to talk to Harrison. Their mission was to convince the governor to stop and agree to peace negotiations the following day. Harrison agreed to the request, even though his subordinates told him that they believed it was a trick. As a precaution against a possible night attack, Harrison ordered his troops to set up camp by the banks of the Tippecanoe River and to post sentries, or guards, in a ring formation.

In this 19th-century wood engraving, the Prophet is holding a torch and giving a speech to inspire his warriors before a battle. He appears to have in his left hand a sacred bundle that he is presenting to the warriors.

Of course, his subordinate officers were right; it was a trick. As the sun began to set, the Prophet, wearing a necklace of deer hooves and carrying strings of sacred beans, went among the warriors. He told them that the Master of Life had given him great medicine that would guarantee them victory. He predicted that he would cause rain to come that would dampen the Long Knives' gunpowder, making it useless for their muzzle loaders. And, while the night would hide them from the Long Knives, the warriors would find the camp to be as bright as day. He also warned them that they must find and kill Harrison. If they did not, the Long Knives would never be defeated. He finished by saying that once Harrison was dead, his troops "would run and hide in the grass" like frightened creatures.

A Night Attack

Buoyed by these and other assurances, the warriors silently advanced and began surrounding the army camp. The attack was scheduled to begin two hours before dawn. One hundred warriors, selected for their stalking skills, would infiltrate the camp and try to kill Harrison before the main attack was launched. If they were discovered, they were to shout war cries, which would be answered by war cries from the warriors outside the camp, who would then attack. The result, it was hoped, would be sufficient confusion and panic to ensure Indian victory.

The result, it was hoped, would be sufficient confusion and panic to ensure Indian victory.

As the Indians got into position, a cold rain began to fall. The warriors saw that the troops had built several large bonfires in the camp. The light from these fires diminished the sentries' night vision while it allowed the warriors to clearly see their enemies' positions. Encouraged by the fact that two of the Prophet's predictions had come true, the chosen warriors began infiltrating the camp.

Harrison awoke at about 4:15 a.m. and was in the process of getting dressed when a shot suddenly rang out. A sentry at the outermost ring of guard posts had spotted some of the warriors. His warning shot was followed by gunfire from other sentries. Then the camp erupted in chaos as warriors shouted bloodcurdling war cries and as confused, half-dressed soldiers rushed out of tents.

Harrison emerged from his own tent in full uniform and called out for his horse, a light gray mare that had been left saddled for the night. However, it had broken loose in the confusion, and Harrison had to mount a dark stallion that belonged to one of his aides. Accompanied by Colonel Abraham Owen, who was mounted on a white horse, they rode toward the northwestern perimeter of the camp, where the attack was fiercest. The infiltrating warriors had been told the color of

This Currier & Ives lithograph of the Battle of Tippecanoe depicts the close-quarters chaos that defined the fight.

Harrison's horse. In the darkness, Owen's white horse looked gray. Two warriors, mistaking Owens for Harrison, shot the colonel, killing him. Moments later those warriors were shot dead.

The battle escalated into a bitter confrontation, with Harrison rushing from one part of the camp to another to rally his men. The Indians fought hard, and for a while it seemed they would overcome the Long Knives. But though the troops' defensive lines had bent, they never broke. When dawn appeared, the Indians melted back into the marshes and nearby woods.

The Battle of Tippecanoe, as it came to be known, was over.

Aftermath of the Battle

During the battle, the Prophet had taken up position on a nearby hill. He continuously chanted and called upon the Master of Life to bring the warriors victory. He was stunned when, shortly after dawn, angry Winnebago warrior allies rushed up to him with the intent to kill him. They accused him of having false medicine and deceiving them. They told him that instead of running away in panic, the Long Knives had fought fiercely.

After spending a day tending to their wounded and reorganizing the camp, Harrison's troops marched on Prophetstown. They entered a village deserted of everyone except an old woman who was too frail to move. The soldiers went through the village and took a variety of household items and other goods. What they couldn't carry away, they burned. Wigwams and more than five thousand bushels of corn and beans were set afire.

Tactically, the Battle of Tippecanoe was a draw. Harrison's army of about a thousand men suffered 188 casualties, including 62 who were killed. The Indian force was as many as seven hundred warriors—about fifty of whom died and eighty more than were wounded.

During the Battle of Tippecanoe, Harrison rode a dark-colored horse belonging to one of his aides, not a white one as shown in this c. 1840 Currier & Ives lithograph.

More importantly, the battle destroyed the Prophet's reputation and was a setback for Tecumseh and his plans for a pan-tribal confederacy. The Prophet would live for twenty-five more years, dying in 1836. But his impact on history and his influence among the Indians ended at Tippecanoe on November 7, 1811.

Prophecy Fulfilled

Before Tippecanoe, Tecumseh had used the growing power of his brother to build his confederacy. Now, Tecumseh would have to continue his efforts on his own. But a fluke of nature changed everything. On December 16, the first of what would be a series of earthquakes struck and leveled every structure in the American settlement New Madrid, located near the border of what is now Missouri and Tennessee. Though New Madrid was the epicenter of the earthquakes, the shockwaves were felt by anyone living within several hundred miles of it. This included the tribes that Tecumseh had visited just two months earlier—when he had said he would stamp his foot and "shake down every house in Tuckhabatchee."

It was an extraordinary coincidence. Even today, scientists, with all of their sensitive instruments, cannot make exact predictions of when an earthquake will strike. Tecumseh was the lucky recipient of one of nature's unpredictable occurrences.

The New Madrid earthquakes of 1811 seemed to realize Tecumseh's earlier threat as it struck down many villages. This 19th-century woodcut print depicts tree trunks and other wreckage piled along a riverbank as a result of the earthquakes.

To all Indians, from doubters to followers, the message was clear: Tecumseh's medicine was supremely powerful. The Great Spirit stood with him. The setback that Tecumseh suffered as a result of his brother's defeat at Tippecanoe had been overcome. Tecumseh

The New Madrid Earthquakes

The New Madrid earthquakes were a series of more than two thousand earthquakes and aftershocks that lasted for four and a half months, from December 1811 to April 1812. The earthquakes got their name from the town of New Madrid—a settlement located beside the Mississippi River on the border between Missouri and Tennessee and over the center of the earthquakes. The most powerful of the quakes were later estimated to be at least 8.0 on the **Richter scale**—more powerful than the great San Francisco earthquake of 1906. The earthquakes were felt as far away as Canada, New York, New Orleans, and Washington, D.C. They directly affected more than 1.5 million square miles in what later became twenty-one states from Kansas to Virginia and Louisiana to Michigan. The earthquakes were so strong that they caused the Mississippi River to temporarily run backward. Though no one knows how many people died during the earthquakes, the total was likely low because few people lived in the area at the time. The region is still an active earthquake zone, and scientists predict that there is up to a 40 percent chance that a major earthquake will occur within the next fifty years.

The etching *Scene of the Great Earthquake in the West* depicts the incredible upheaval of the Mississippi River caused by the New Madrid earthquakes. In some places, the river rose thirty feet and ran backward.

sent out new messengers to tribes near and far, calling for them to join his confederacy and prepare to fight the Long Knives. Indians began to flock to Prophetstown in greater numbers than ever before. Tecumseh even found himself welcoming Sioux warriors from the distant Dakota plains.

More Threats

Tecumseh began making plans to travel north to Fort Malden in Canada to convince the Wyandot, Ottawa, and Ojibwa tribes living along the Detroit River to join him. News of this trip reached American officials in the frontier territories, and they reacted with alarm. Tensions between Great Britain and the United States were finally reaching a breaking point. An army was ordered to Fort Detroit to defend the vulnerable border with Canada. Tecumseh was warned that if he made his trip to Fort Malden, the American government would consider the move a hostile act and send that army against him.

Tecumseh refused to let this threat worry him. At the same time, he did not want to suffer another defeat like the one that occurred at Tippecanoe. He went to Fort Wayne in Indiana Territory on June 17, 1812, to soothe the fears of the new government agent responsible for Indian affairs, Benjamin Stickney. The meeting solved nothing. Stickney was not fooled by Tecumseh's speech about wanting only peace, and Tecumseh was not intimidated by Stickney's threats to use the army in Fort Detroit to stop him. When Tecumseh left for Fort Malden on June 21, he refused to shake Stickney's hand.

When he arrived at Fort Malden at the end of June, he discovered that the United States and Great Britain had declared war on each other. The War of 1812 had begun.

CHAPTER 11

War in the West

A more sagacious or more a gallant warrior does not, I believe, exist.

—*Major General Sir Isaac Brock*

In early July 1812, an American army more than two thousand strong left Fort Detroit. Leading it was a hero of the American Revolution, Brigadier General William Hull, who was also serving as the governor of Michigan Territory. On July 12, they crossed the border into Canada. The invasion of Canada had begun. Against this army the British could only assemble a mixed force led by Lieutenant Colonel Thomas Bligh St. George. It contained about three hundred regular troops, six hundred militia, and Indian warriors of varying numbers and reliability.

The British and their colonists of Upper Canada were tense and afraid. They were few in number and far from the large garrisons in Toronto and Montreal that were hundreds of miles to the east. Any defense they attempted would be crushed, and the region would quickly be conquered.

An American Army Invades Canada

The Canadians' fears appeared to come true when Hull's army occupied the town of Sandwich. Hull issued a proclamation that his army had come to liberate the Canadians from the "tyranny and oppression" of the British. He also made a blood-chilling threat: "No white man found fighting by the side of an Indian will be taken prisoner. Instant destruction will be his lot." Panic swept the region. Hundreds of Canadians were so intimidated by Hull's threats that they either surrendered or deserted their militia.

On July 12, [the American army] crossed the border into Canada. The invasion of Canada had begun.

But the only effect Hull's threats had on Tecumseh was to spur him into greater action. Tecumseh had under his command almost four hundred warriors, who were eager to fight. St. George knew that his small British force could not properly support the Indians if they attacked Hull's army. Repeatedly he had urged Tecumseh to hold back his warriors. On July 16, American troops captured a bridge over the Aux Canard River and were now in an excellent position to conquer Fort Malden. St. George had no other choice; he finally agreed with Tecumseh. Now was the time to fight.

That evening, Tecumseh's warriors put on their war paint and danced their war dances in preparation for a major battle the next day. Shortly after dawn, the warriors advanced, eager for battle, followed by their British allies. When they reached the bridge, they discovered to their surprise that the American troops were gone! For some unknown reason, Hull had called them back.

Fort Malden became a key staging base for British forces based in Upper Canada during the War of 1812. Shown here is an undated postcard of Fort Malden, which is now a national historic site of Canada.

The reason behind their bloodless victory was that Hull, a brave soldier in the American Revolution, was now an old man and had become a timid commander on the frontier during the War of 1812. In a letter to his wife, Major James Denny, one of Hull's subordinates, wrote, "Our general is losing all the confidence he had in the army." But in judging Hull, one has to remember that he was burdened by a number of very real problems: He was in a remote location where reinforcement was difficult, and his long lines of supply and communications could be easily cut off. But it was thought that he let those concerns become fears so great that he became too paralyzed to act.

Though he was a hero of the American Revolution, William Hull proved a timid commander during the War of 1812. There were so few experienced officers in the U.S. Army that the government was forced to turn to overage men like Hull to command troops.

The same was not true of Tecumseh. Every patrol that the Americans sent out was attacked by his warriors. The **skirmishes** were small, but their impact was far-reaching. Morale among Tecumseh's warriors soared. Discontent in the American camp increased. Tribes in the region who said they were neutral or who had sided with the Americans now began to reconsider.

Battle at Brownstown

Tecumseh succeeded in convincing three pro-American Wyandot villages to switch sides. This was a diplomatic triumph that suddenly placed Hull's invasion of Canada in jeopardy. These villages were located on the only road that connected Hull to his supply and communications base in Fort Detroit. With those villages now in his hands, Tecumseh could easily isolate the American army. This threat finally forced Hull to act. He ordered a powerful force of two hundred militia led by Major Thomas Van Horne to travel south. The force was to open the route and link with a small supply convoy traveling north from Fort Detroit. To prevent this from happening, Tecumseh went after them and took with him twenty-five warriors.

Tecumseh was not worried that he was outnumbered more than eight to one. He first attacked the southern convoy, captured its supplies, and forced the survivors to retreat. Then he set up an ambush for the larger force near Brownstown, one of the villages that had switched sides. The site was along a shallow creek crossing north of town, where the Americans would be most vulnerable to attack. With his warriors well hidden in the fields and forests along the riverbank, Tecumseh waited to spring his trap. He did not have long to wait.

Tecumseh was not worried that he was outnumbered more than eight to one.

The unsuspecting Americans arrived, marching in two columns. The columns converged so that they could wade the narrow crossing together.

The lead men in the column were just fifty yards away from the Indians when Tecumseh gave the order to fire.

The suddenness of the attack stunned the Americans. Their ranks erupted into chaos as wounded and frightened horses threw their riders and bolted to safety. The foot soldiers struggled to wade back to shore, retreating under heavy and accurate fire. At one point early in the battle, some of the better-trained members of Van Horne's force tried to re-form into a defensive line, but that effort failed. The militia disintegrated into a panic-stricken mob that abandoned its wagons and weapons. Van Horne lost about a quarter of his men. For several days, survivors straggled into Fort Detroit, about ten miles away, their tales of the disaster adding to the garrison's gloom.

Tecumseh had scored a remarkable victory. Crowning that success was the discovery of a mailbag in one of the wagons that contained a letter from General Hull to his superiors in Washington. It revealed that Hull believed he was surrounded by thousands of Indians, that his situation was becoming critical, and that he was afraid he would be overwhelmed if he did not get reinforcements.

A few days after Tecumseh's victory, Hull ordered his army back to Fort Detroit. Only a small force was left behind to guard the retreat. The American invasion of Canada in the West was finished.

But Hull's problems were not. In fact, they would soon get worse.

General Brock Arrives

Tecumseh knew that the time was ripe to take the next step and capture Fort Detroit. But to do that, he needed British help. Fortunately for him, Major General Isaac Brock arrived at Fort Malden in August 1812, leading an army of three hundred men. Brock was a tall, handsome, highly intelligent man. He was full of dash and vigor and had earned the admiration of the men under him. In addition to being

This line drawing by Charles William Jefferys depicts General Isaac Brock on horseback. Brock was an intelligent and gifted British commander.

a military commander, he was also the lieutenant governor of Upper Canada. This made him the most powerful British official west of Lake Erie. His arrival showed everyone how important the campaign in the West was for the British.

Tecumseh and Brock met briefly on the evening of August 13. Because the hour was well after midnight, they exchanged greetings and agreed to have a full meeting the following day. During the council on August 14, Tecumseh heard words that filled his heart with joy. Brock wanted to capture Fort Detroit! What he didn't know was that Brock's decision was in direct conflict with the orders of his superior, Governor-General Sir George Prevost, who believed the risk was too great and had ordered Brock *not* to attempt an attack on Fort Detroit. But Brock knew of Hull's letter and believed that he could force Hull to surrender through either bluff or battle.

When their meeting ended, Tecumseh happily cried, "This is a man!" Tecumseh had finally met a British officer who did not want to wait until he had more men and supplies. Brock was ready to fight now with what he had. The two left to prepare for the assault on Fort Detroit.

The historic meeting between Tecumseh and General Brock is depicted in this colored line drawing by Charles William Jefferys. Brock gave Tecumseh hope that at long last the Shawnee chief would be able to make his dream of a pan-tribal confederacy a reality.

Battle at Fort Detroit

Brock began his campaign by writing a letter to General Hull, calling for him to surrender. But Hull rejected the surrender. The two sides were pretty evenly matched. Hull's garrison in the fort totaled about thirteen hundred men, and the fort was sturdily built. He also had several powerful cannons and ample supplies and ammunition. The combined force led by Brock and Tecumseh numbered about the same. Brock also had several cannons, including those on the ships that had ferried him and his men to Fort Malden.

The attack began shortly after dawn, on August 15, 1812, with an exchange of cannon fire. Brock cleverly marched and countermarched his uniformed troops in front of the American lines. These back-and-forth movements caused the Americans to believe that his force was larger than it really was. British cannon fire was accurate and caused numerous casualties on Hull's side. American cannon fire was poorly aimed. In one case, a battery of three cannons located in a forward position and defending the fort was found abandoned before it had fired a shot. Tecumseh and his warriors added to the Americans'

Fort Detroit was originally a trading fort founded by French explorers. This drawing shows how the fort looked in 1749. Its location on the Detroit River, amid the Great Lakes, made it one of the most important forts on the frontier during the War of 1812.

Major General William Hull (1753–1825)

Few men in history had as unfortunate an ending of a respected career as William Hull. Hull was a hero of the American Revolution who fought with distinction in numerous battles, including Trenton, Princeton, Saratoga, Monmouth, and Stony Point. His courage earned him the praise of General George Washington and the thanks of Congress—high honors in those days. In 1805, he was appointed the territorial governor of Michigan by President Thomas Jefferson. When the War of 1812 broke out, Hull was recalled to military service and ordered to conduct an invasion of Upper Canada. The failure of his invasion and his surrender of Fort Detroit to General Brock and Tecumseh caused him to be **court-martialed**. Hull retired to Massachusetts and attempted to clear his reputation by writing two books about what happened. Historians have since agreed that Hull was made a **scapegoat** for the disaster that occurred in the frontier.

General Hull was one of the heroes of the Battle of Princeton. A scene from that battle is depicted here in the painting *Battle of Princeton* by American Revolution artist John Trumbull.

confusion by conducting small skirmish attacks that also made his force appear larger than it was.

The next morning, at about 10 a.m., the cannon inside the fort stopped firing. A white flag appeared over a wall of the fort. General Brock ordered a couple of aides to ride to the American lines. Hull was ready to surrender not just the forces in the fort but also his entire army—a total of almost 2,200 men!

For Tecumseh, the capture of Fort Detroit was a high point in his cause. He and his men celebrated long into the night.

General Hull is shown in this 19th-century engraving contemplating his surrender to General Brock after Brock's masterful siege of Fort Detroit.

In his report of the victory, General Brock singled Tecumseh out for praise, calling him "the Wellington of the Indians"—a reference comparing him to the great British general the Duke of Wellington.

With the western frontier secured, General Brock prepared to return east where an American invasion of Canada near the Niagara River loomed. Shortly before he left, he wrote a letter to the British prime minister, Lord Liverpool, recounting his recent experience and urging the government to provide as much assistance as possible to the Indian cause in the West. In the letter he wrote of Tecumseh, "A more sagacious or more a gallant warrior does not, I believe, exist."

Tecumseh had been instrumental in helping the British keep possession of Canada. The question now was, Were the British willing to provide the same amount of help to their ally?

Major General Sir Isaac Brock (1769–1812)

One of Britain's most successful generals in the War of 1812 was born on the British island of Guernsey to a middle-class family. Isaac Brock joined the British army in 1785 and served in a variety of posts on the Caribbean islands and in Europe before being sent to Canada in 1802. He rose in rank and administrative authority over the years. When the War of 1812 started, he was a major general and the lieutenant governor of Upper Canada. This made him one of the three most powerful men in Canada. It was thanks to his energetic efforts that Canada was able to resist repeated invasions by American troops. He greatly respected Tecumseh and did everything he could to support the chief's confederacy efforts. Brock's most successful achievement was the capture of Fort Detroit, which ended American attempts to conquer the region and make it a part of the United States. Brock was killed during the Battle of Queenston Heights (also known as Queenstown Heights) on October 13, 1812, a British victory that successfully ended American attempts to conquer Lower Canada.

General Brock, an exceptional military man shown in this undated portrait, was greatly admired by Tecumseh.

CHAPTER 12

A Man of Courage and Mercy

I could not understand his language, but his gestures and manner satisfied me that he was on the side of mercy.

—Leslie Combs, an American prisoner

In late 1812, Tecumseh's health failed, and he remained bedridden for months. It is unknown why he was sick. Perhaps it was a lingering cold or the flu, or perhaps he was suffering from an extreme case of mental and physical exhaustion. He was in his forties at that point, and though he kept up to date with news, he was unable to participate in any of the major battles going on during the winter. Finally, in April 1813, he was back in action.

Battle at Fort Meigs

Tecumseh's first major battle was at the head of a force of fourteen hundred warriors. He was assisting British Brigadier General Henry Procter in an attack against the American outpost of Fort Meigs, located near the mouth of the Maumee River in northwestern Ohio. The fort successfully remained in American hands. But an army of reinforcements sent by Tecumseh's old nemesis, General William Henry Harrison, was badly beaten and a large number of prisoners were taken. Tecumseh fought bravely

In this detail of an 1840 lithograph by George Endicott, General Harrison directs cannon fire in the defense of Fort Meigs. Harrison succeeded in keeping the fort in American hands.

and with great skill during the battle, but it was the events that followed at Fort Miami that would make him a legend.

Following the battle at Fort Meigs, General Procter had sent the American prisoners under an armed escort of fifty soldiers to the former British outpost of Fort Miami. The fort was partially in ruins, having been abandoned not long after the incident of 1794 in which the British garrison had refused to provide refuge for warriors following the Battle of Fallen Timbers. Tecumseh was still on the battlefield, reorganizing his warriors, when a frantic messenger arrived from Fort Miami urgently calling for his help. A large number of angry warriors had gathered at the fort and were massacring the prisoners!

A Rescue from Violence

During the march to the fort, the guards had been unable to prevent warriors from hounding the prisoners and stripping them of clothing or other items that caught their fancy. Trouble escalated when the warriors and their prisoners, along with a small group of British soldiers, arrived at the fort. The prisoners were forced to run between two lines of Indians who were armed with clubs and other weapons and who beat the prisoners severely as they ran the gauntlet. The British soldiers had hoped to guard the prisoners

Brigadier General Henry Procter (c. 1763–1822)

Henry Procter was the son of a surgeon in the British army. He served as a junior officer in the British army during the final months of the American Revolution. Following the war, he was stationed in Canada. When the War of 1812 started, he was a colonel serving in the western part of the territory under Major General Sir Isaac Brock.

Though Procter had proved himself capable of drilling and maintaining the discipline of his troops, he revealed himself to be less competent as a combat leader. He also proved inefficient in organizing the transport of troops and supplies.

After Brock was transferred east, Procter, now a brigadier general, was placed in command of the British western frontier. This appointment proved disastrous. He was court-martialed for the conduct of his retreat following the British defeat at the Battle of the Thames. This effectively ended his military career. He retired to England in 1815 and died there in 1822.

once they were within the crumbling walls of the fort. But that hope ended brutally when one British soldier was killed trying to protect an American prisoner.

The slaughter soon began with terrified prisoners trying to avoid being shot or tomahawked to death. In the middle of this terrible scene, Tecumseh dramatically rode into the

A large number of angry warriors had gathered at the fort and were massacring the prisoners!

fort. Leslie Combs, one of the American prisoners, later wrote that he saw a "noble looking chief" walk "hastily into the midst of the savages" and jump to a "high point of the wall" so that he could

This 1877 engraving depicts Tecumseh saving American captives at Fort Miami from being slaughtered by Indian warriors. The event as illustrated, however, is highly distorted. Procter, shown watching passively, was not present, and it is unlikely that Tecumseh was wearing a British-like uniform.

be seen by everyone. It was Tecumseh. Combs wrote, "I could not understand his language, but his gestures and manner satisfied me that he was on the side of mercy."

The details of what happened next differ, but all stories end in agreement. The warriors stopped their assault. Remaining true to his principles of protecting prisoners from being killed or tortured, Tecumseh had saved the remaining Americans. The nobility of this gesture made him a hero even to his American enemies. John Richardson, one of the survivors, later said, "Never did Tecumseh shine more truly than on this occasion."

Tecumseh's reputation was at its peak in the weeks following the battle at Fort Meigs. But Tecumseh's success in the Old Northwest was overshadowed by American victories elsewhere. Slowly the tide was turning against him.

CHAPTER 13

The Final Fight

Father, tell your men to be firm and all will be well.

On September 10, 1813, an American fleet under Commodore Oliver Hazard Perry defeated the British fleet in the Battle of Lake Erie. This battle was a decisive turning point in the war in the West. On the surface, it appeared that nothing had changed the situation in the Detroit region. British General Procter commanded the largest military force in the area. In addition to his own army of about thirteen hundred troops, he was aided by almost twelve hundred warriors commanded by Tecumseh. This did not include the nearby militia he could call upon as well as other fortifications and his cannons. But Procter was worried that they could still be cut off by the American navy that now had the upper hand in the Great Lakes.

Crisis Between Allies

Perhaps things would have been different if General Brock had remained in command. But Brock was dead, killed in the Battle of Queenston Heights near the Niagara River in October of 1812. Though their relationship had started out well, Tecumseh discovered to his disgust that Procter was no Brock. In the middle of September, Procter ordered Fort Malden dismantled and abandoned. When he heard the news, Tecumseh was astonished. Procter was retreating like a coward; there was not even a single Long Knife soldier in the area to attack him!

The Battle of Lake Erie

One of the most important battles in the War of 1812 was the Battle of Lake Erie, which is also known as the Battle of Put-in-Bay—the part of the lake where the battle occurred. On September 10, 1813, an American fleet of nine ships under the command of Commodore Oliver Hazard Perry attacked and defeated a British squadron led by Captain Robert Barclay. The battle was unusual in that both sides fought in ships that were hastily constructed out of freshly cut wood, which made them prone to leaking. The ships on both sides were manned by a mixed group composed mostly of men who had little ship experience. The American victory cleared the way for the land campaign planned by General William Henry Harrison. It also gave a huge boost to American morale, which was at a low point. Perry's letter announcing his victory contained a line that made him famous: "We have met the enemy and they are ours."

This c. 1911 illustration of the Battle of Lake Erie shows American commodore Oliver Hazard Perry traveling to another ship after his flagship *Lawrence* was sunk. Perry's leadership led to a decisive American victory that made General Harrison's advance into Canada possible.

General Brock's death at the Battle of Queenston Heights, as depicted in this undated painting, caused Tecumseh to lose his most important ally. Procter's support would prove to be a poor substitute in the subsequent weeks.

Tecumseh angrily demanded and received a meeting with the British general. Shortly after the meeting began, Tecumseh correctly guessed two things: The British were more concerned about protecting Canada than they were of helping Tecumseh and his confederacy, and Procter had no stomach for fighting.

Realizing he had nothing to lose, Tecumseh stepped forward in front of the assembled British troops and Indian warriors. His goal was to either stir—or shame—Procter into helping them fight. He began by reminding Procter of the help the Indians gave the British during the American Revolution and of the British government's betrayal in the Treaty of Paris that ended the war.

Tecumseh then moved on to the present conflict. He reminded Procter that he and his warriors were eager to fight, but that Procter kept telling them to wait. Tecumseh may or may not have known that Procter was unpopular with his own subordinates, who shared Tecumseh's disgust over the general's timid commands and lack of leadership. They were greatly enjoying Procter's discomfort when Tecumseh came to the main point of his

In this undated illustration, Tecumseh is shown talking to General Procter. It is a testament to Tecumseh's dedication that he did everything he could to inspire Procter to be a more aggressive commander.

argument: "We see you are drawing back, and we are sorry to see [you're] doing so without seeing the enemy. We must compare [your] conduct to a fat animal that carries its tail upon its back, but when affrightened, it drops it between its legs and runs off."

Ripples of laughter broke out among the warriors. When this part of the speech was translated, Procter flushed a deep red as his ears echoed with additional laughter from the British troops.

Having challenged Procter's courage, Tecumseh now sought to shame him to fight. He made his final challenge: "Father! You have got the arms and ammunition that our Great Father [the king] sent for [us]. If you have an idea of going away, give them to us, and you may go."

If Procter was not prepared to fight, then Tecumseh and his warriors would fight—and die—alone. All they asked was that the British leave their weapons with them so that each could die as a warrior should, bravely in battle, defending his land.

Procter had many faults as a general, but he was correct in one thing. Their position left them vulnerable to being cut off and attacked from the rear. However, Procter's credibility was so low that saying so would have been a colossal mistake. Prudently, Procter said he would meet with Tecumseh two days later to discuss a new plan of action.

A New Plan

During that time, Procter stared at his maps and read the latest reports of the military situation on the Great Lakes and elsewhere in the West. It was clear to him that with the American naval division in control of the lower Great Lakes, his enemies now had the initiative. No matter which way he looked at it, the only solution for him was to retreat. But how far, and to where?

Meanwhile, Tecumseh watched the activity of his British allies with suspicion. While he waited for Procter, he saw British soldiers take guns, ammunition, and supplies out of Fort Malden for transport up the Thames River. This abandonment spoke loudly to the chief who had witnessed brave words followed by cowardly actions by the British earlier in his life.

. . . Tecumseh watched the activity of his British allies with suspicion.

Colonel Matthew Elliott, who had known Tecumseh for many years and was the trader who had earlier passed British arms to Tecumseh, was perhaps the Shawnee chief's only true friend and ally. Over the years, Elliott had proven himself useful to the British in their relations with the Indians in the region. The value of his close relations with the Indians, especially Tecumseh, was instrumental in causing the British to give him the rank of colonel. But now, Elliott was in an impossible position. Lacking any real authority, he could only advise and plead for Tecumseh's patience. As far as Tecumseh was concerned, though, time had run out. If the British wanted to run away like cowards, so be it. Tecumseh's warriors were becoming so impatient and angry that they even threatened to kill Elliott.

Procter met Tecumseh on September 20 and recognized how close things were to spinning out of control. Unrolling a large map of the Detroit region onto a table, and with Elliott interpreting, Procter explained the military situation in detail to Tecumseh.

Within minutes, tensions began to ease. Tecumseh knew how to read a map and, according to one of Procter's aides, Captain John Hall, he "asked many questions and made several shrewd remarks in reference to the map." Then Procter explained that he planned to establish a new line of defense at a place west of Lake St. Clair called Chatham, where the Thames River forks, because that landscape offered a better defensive position than the land around Fort Malden.

Reassured by this news, Tecumseh agreed that it was a better location. The meeting concluded with Tecumseh requesting time to discuss what he had learned with the other chiefs in order to obtain their consent. Within two hours, Tecumseh returned and, according to Procter, said that he "had brought the greater portion of the chiefs and nations into my proposal."

The next day, the retreat east by most of Tecumseh's army and followers began. The last two to leave were Tecumseh and Colonel Elliott. They sadly watched smoke rise from Fort Malden and a variety of outbuildings that the British had put to the torch. Soon the structure Tecumseh had come to regard as a symbol of his confederacy's alliance with the British would be in ashes.

Finding a New Defensive Position

Six days later, British rear-guard scouts saw American ships carrying General Harrison's army of more than three thousand men arrive.

The distance from Fort Malden to the new defensive position was thirty miles. Rain had turned the primitive, dirt-covered roads into muddy trails. Most of the British troops, traveling along the southern bank, were able to cover the distance within three days.

Tecumseh's group, traveling along the northern bank, was slowed by the warriors' exhausted families, who were transporting all their possessions. Regard for Procter began eroding during the retreat. More often than not, Procter was unavailable because he was traveling in his carriage far ahead of his troops. This caused rumors to circulate that he was abandoning his men.

Whatever goodwill Procter had inspired in his conference on September 20 evaporated when Tecumseh reached the fork of the Thames River that the British general claimed would be their new line of defense. He saw four cannons haphazardly positioned and a small hut containing just a few muskets. There were no trenches, no waist-high walls of earth to protect defenders. There was nothing. Even General Procter was gone!

Tecumseh was thunderstruck and furious. He seethed over this latest example of Procter's empty promises.

Tecumseh was thunderstruck and furious. He seethed over this latest example of Procter's empty promises.

The truth, however, was that Procter had not abandoned his troops and Tecumseh. Rather, after a final inspection of the site, he had decided that it was unsuitable for defense, and he was searching for a different location. But instead of keeping Tecumseh informed of his actions and decisions, he had gone off in search of a better place—without even telling his own men!

Losing Heart

Once again, Colonel Elliott was the target of warrior anger and he suffered a new round of torture-filled death threats. But with the American troops near, a more important decision had to be made. Should they stay and fight, or should they continue to retreat upriver? Tecumseh wanted to stay, but the majority of Elliott's troops were on the other side of the river and, lacking boats, could not cross and reinforce the warriors. Tecumseh resigned himself to the fact that he'd have to continue retreating. On October 4, the dispirited Indians continued upriver.

Tecumseh had faced and overcome many problems and challenges that would have overwhelmed a lesser man. But with this latest setback, even his great self-confidence was shaken. In fact, it proved too much for some tribes in his group. A few began to desert. There was nothing Tecumseh could do to stop them. Within hours, the group traveling upriver shrank to just five hundred warriors together with their families. He took heart from the fact that this group had followed him almost from the very beginning. Tecumseh resolved to continue the fight, come what may.

Preparing for Battle

When Tecumseh arrived that evening at the British and Indian camp that Procter had set up near the Thames River, he knew that the following day would decide things once and for all. The thought of battling the Americans after all the retreats inspired him. He spent several hours among his warriors, reminiscing with them and buoying their spirits. A number of warriors later said that they sensed that Tecumseh knew his cause was lost and that he would die in battle the next day. Even so, they all remembered that he never appeared depressed, just thoughtful.

The morning of October 5 was bright, and the morning chill soon gave way to sunny warmth. The fair weather further lifted the spirits of the warriors as they prepared for battle. Tecumseh and Procter agreed that Tecumseh's warriors would take up position

This reenactor is wearing a reproduction of a typical uniform worn by British foot soldiers during the War of 1812. The bright red and white uniform made a soldier a prime target.

on the right flank, between two swamps, where the terrain favored the ambush style of Indian fighting.

Unfortunately, Procter's poor military skill revealed itself with the condition and positioning of his troops. His men were exhausted after all their marching. They had not eaten a real meal for the past day and a half. Most of their ammunition had been lost. They had only one small cannon with a few rounds of shot. The troops were poorly placed in an open field, and they had no fortifications of any kind to protect them. Plus, their red and white uniforms, though dirty from the recent marching, made excellent targets for the American marksmen.

At noon, scouts brought word that Harrison's army would soon arrive. Tecumseh appeared to greet the news with pleasure, as if happy that the waiting was finally over. John Richardson, one of the British officers who fought in the battle, later wrote, "Only a few minutes before the clang of the American bugles was heard ringing through the forest . . . Tecumseh passed along our line. . . . He was dressed in his usual deer skin dress, which admirably displayed his light yet sinewy figure, and in his handkerchief, rolled as

This undated image shows what appears to be an elderly Tecumseh. In 1813, Tecumseh was certainly feeling the burden of his efforts. Despite all his work to rally the tribes, he had few warriors with him for what became the Battle of the Thames.

a turban over his brow, was placed a handsome white ostrich feather. . . . He pressed the hand of each officer he passed, made some remarks in Shawnee appropriate to the occasion which was sufficiently understood by the expressive signs accompanying them, and then passed away forever from our view."

Tecumseh approached Procter and, with Elliott interpreting, warned the British general that his troops were positioned too closely together and that the soldiers manning the cannon had to be particularly courageous because they would be the primary target for the Americans. Then, seeing the grim expression on Procter's face, he said, "Father, tell your men to be firm and all will be well. . . . Father, have a big heart." Then he left to join his warriors.

The Battle of the Thames Begins

Harrison and his American army arrived at about mid-afternoon. Earlier his scouts had warned him that Tecumseh's warriors were well hidden on his left flank. Harrison decided to make his main attack on the British. In their exposed position, they were more vulnerable. If he succeeded in defeating them, he figured, the Indians would lose heart and quickly leave the battle.

After ordering part of his infantry to protect his left flank by slowly advancing toward the Indians' position, Harrison ordered his men forward.

The sound of American bugles filled the air, followed by the thundering of Harrison's cavalry. Then came the crackle of volley after volley from American rifles. The battlefield was quickly filled with thick clouds of black gunpowder smoke that burned the throat and hid the troops from one another.

Within five minutes of the firing of the first volley, the British lines collapsed. The defending infantry fired at most three volleys before abandoning their position. As for the soldiers manning the cannon, they deserted without firing a single shot.

General Procter made a halfhearted attempt to stop the attack. Then he turned his horse around and galloped away, outdistancing his men.

Death of Tecumseh

While General Procter was abandoning his troops and allies to their fate, Tecumseh was carrying on the battle. He drove back Harrison's flanking force—even after additional troops reinforced them. Tecumseh seemed to be everywhere, his face covered in red and black war paint, a British medal proudly resting on his chest. He yelled encouragement to his warriors, fired a couple of quick shots at the Long Knives, then dashed to another position to offer support.

It was during one of these dashes that an American soldier saw him, took aim, and fired. Tecumseh fell, mortally wounded in the chest. One soldier later recalled that as soon as that happened, the warriors nearby "gave the loudest yells I ever heard from human beings and that ended the fight." Within minutes, word of Tecumseh's death swept through the warriors' ranks, and the surviving Indians abandoned the fight and retreated to safety.

The Battle of the Thames was over. Harrison's victory

Tecumseh was a dynamic force during the Battle of the Thames. This illustration shows him defiantly raising his tomahawk to rally his warriors.

This Currier & Ives print from 1846, *Death of Tecumseh*, is a fanciful image of how the Shawnee chief fell in battle.

decisively won for the United States the War of 1812 in the West. And with no chief possessing the stature needed to carry on with Tecumseh's dream, Harrison's victory also meant the end of Tecumseh's pan-tribal confederacy.

A number of legends surround the fate of Tecumseh's body—some quite gruesome, with skin and body parts taken and displayed as trophies. But no one knows the truth. All that is known for certain is that he died the way he wished—as a warrior in battle against his enemies.

Years later, in 1830, two Americans visited the old battlefield. At a site where a local guide claimed Tecumseh was buried, one of them, Daniel R. Dunihue, took out a paper and pencil and began writing:

> *Sleep on brave chief! Sleep on in Glory's arms!*
> *Freed from men's malice, and from War's alarms;*
> *Distinguished savage, great in mind and soul,*
> *Rest here in peace, while ceaseless ages roll.*

Glossary

almanac—a handbook containing important dates and statistical information such as tide tables, seasonal temperatures, and planting and harvesting schedules.

armistice—a truce.

casualties—persons killed or injured in war.

cavalry—soldiers who fight on horseback.

commissioners—persons appointed to a position of responsibility by a government.

confederacy—a group joined together by formal agreement for a common purpose.

court-martialed—put on trial by a military court for an offense under military law.

diplomacy—the skillful management of relations between countries.

frontiers—wilderness areas that contain few or no settlers.

fundamentalism—a usually religious belief that seeks to follow rigid principles.

garrisoned—being provided troops in a fort or town for its defense.

gut—fiber made from animal intestines and used by Native Americans to make bowstrings.

infantry—foot soldiers.

midwives—women trained to assist in childbirth.

neutrality—the status of nations or people who do not help or support either of two sides in a conflict.

nomadic—being constantly on the move, traveling from one place to another, usually seasonally in search of food and water.

palisades—fences of stakes, especially for defense.

pan-tribal—containing many Native American tribes.

pawns—persons used by others for the users' own purpose.

prophet—someone who predicts future events, often considered a messenger of a divine spirit.

ransomed—to have paid money for the release of a prisoner.

renegade—a rebellious person acting on his own, often unlawfully.

reservations—lands set aside for a group of people.

Richter scale—a numerical scale used to measure the strength of an earthquake. A 6.0 or above indicates a major earthquake.

scapegoat—a person blamed for the wrongdoing or failure of others.

scouts—people, usually soldiers, sent to gather information about an enemy's location.

siege—a military operation in which enemy forces are surrounded and supplies are cut off, forcing a surrender.

skirmishes—short, quick battles, usually between two small groups.

surveyors—people who use special instruments and tools to measure and map the land.

Trojan-Horse trick—a person or thing that secretly brings about the downfall of an enemy. The term is based on the story of how hidden Greeks entered the city of Troy in a hollow wooden horse and overran the city.

wampum—small beads that were shaped out of quahog shells by Native Americans and were used as money or to make ceremonial objects, such as decorative belts.

Bibliography

Books

Borneman, Walter R. *1812: The War that Forged a Nation*. New York: Harper Perennial, 2005.

Edmunds, R. David. *The Shawnee Prophet*. Lincoln, Neb.: University of Nebraska Press, 1983.

———. *Tecumseh and the Quest for Indian Leadership*. New York: Pearson, Longman, 2007.

Feldman, Jay. *When the Mississippi Ran Backwards: Empire, Intrigue, Murder, and the New Madrid Earthquakes*. New York: Free Press, 2005.

Mattern, Joanne. *The Shawnee Indians*. Mankato, Minn.: Bridgestone Books, 2001.

Sugden, John. *Tecumseh: A Life*. New York: Henry Holt, 1997.

Tebbel, John, and Keith Jennison. *The American Indian Wars*. Edison, N.J.: Castle Books, 2006.

Web Sites

Anonymous. "Historical Narratives of Early Canada." www.uppercanadahistory.ca/1812/18122.html (accessed February 5, 2008).

———. "Tecumseh's Speech of August 11, 1810." www.geocities.com/SouthBeach/Cove/8286/harrison.html (accessed February 1, 2008).

Ruddell, Stephen. "Reminiscences of Tecumseh's Youth." Wisconsin Historical Society Digital Library and Archives, *American Journeys Collection*, pp. 120–133. http://content.wisconsinhistory.org/cdm4/document.php?CISOROOT=/aj&CISOPTR=17916 (accessed February 6, 2008).

Sellars, Jim, ed. "Letters of John Mulherin Ruddell to Lyman Copeland Draper." http://www.ark-us.org/ruddell/ruddell15.html.

Source Notes

The following list identifies the sources of the quoted material found in this book. The first and last few words of each quotation are cited, followed by the source. Complete information on each source can be found in the Bibliography.

Abbreviations:

1812—*1812: The War that Forged a Nation*

AIW—*The American Indian Wars*

HNEC—"Historical Narratives of Early Canada"

PAGE 116 *"gave the loudest . . . ended the fight.":* TAL, p. 374
PAGE 117 *"Sleep on brave . . . ceaseless age roll.":* TAL, p. 380

Image Credits

Archives of Ontario: 61
© Bettmann/CORBIS: 41, 63, 75, 109
© The Gallery Collection/Corbis: 13
© Angelo Hornak/CORBIS: 12
© David Muench/CORBIS: 31
Darke County Historical Society: 46
Simon Collier/billy liar/www.flickr.com: 10
Bert Cozens/Hear and Their/www.flickr.com: 93
Jeff Farmer/Mr Geoff/www.flickr.com: 3
Bart Heird/ChiBart/www.flickr.com: 53
Bill Mattocks/Wigwam Jones/www.flickr.com: 114 (top)
Shannon Blosser-Salisbury/The Pollyanna Society/www.flickr.com: 62
Kevin Stewart/kevystew/www.flickr.com: 37
Hulton Archive/Getty Images: 114 (bottom)
MPI/Getty Images: 8
The Granger Collection, New York: 5, 6, 7, 9, 17, 20, 21, 32, 33, 42, 47, 48, 52, 58, 67, 80, 81, 85, 87, 90, 96, 97, 98, 100, 103, 105, 116
Project Gutenberg Literary Archive Foundation: 101
Library and Archives Canada: 108
Library of Congress: 4, 11, 15, 18, 27, 28, 29, 35, 36, 44, 49, 57, 74, 84, 88, 99, 107, 117
NASA: 56
National Archives and Records Administration: 19
© North Wind/North Wind Picture Archives: 25, 51, 69, 78, 89, 94
Hal Sherman: 23, 24, 43
U.S. Army: 39, 70
Yesterday's Classics LLC: 82
Cover art: Michael Haynes

About the Author

Dwight Jon Zimmerman began his writing career in the comic book industry. He has written stories about such superheroes as Spider-Man, the X-Men, the Incredible Hulk, Iron Man, Superman, Batman, and many others. He has written numerous books and articles about natural history and military history for the adult and young adult markets. His book *First Command: Paths to Leadership* is a young-adult biography about the pivotal experiences in the beginning of the careers of a number of American generals, men, women, and minorities, from George Washington to present day. His most recent book, *The Day the World Exploded*, is the young-adult adaptation of Simon Winchester's best-selling account of the destruction of Krakatoa in 1883. He lives in Brooklyn, New York.

Index

Discover interesting personalities in the Sterling Biographies® series:

Muhammad Ali: *King of the Ring*

Marian Anderson: *A Voice Uplifted*

Neil Armstrong: *One Giant Leap for Mankind*

Alexander Graham Bell: *Giving Voice to the World*

Cleopatra: *Egypt's Last and Greatest Queen*

Christopher Columbus: *The Voyage That Changed the World*

Jacques Cousteau: *A Life Under the Sea*

Davy Crockett: *Frontier Legend*

Marie Curie: *Mother of Modern Physics*

Frederick Douglass: *Rising Up from Slavery*

Amelia Earhart: *A Life in Flight*

Thomas Edison: *The Man Who Lit Up the World*

Albert Einstein: *The Miracle Mind*

Anne Frank: *Hidden Hope*

Benjamin Franklin: *Revolutionary Inventor*

Lou Gehrig: *Iron Horse of Baseball*

Geronimo: *Apache Renegade*

Matthew Henson: *The Quest for the North Pole*

Harry Houdini: *Death-Defying Showman*

Thomas Jefferson: *Architect of Freedom*

Joan of Arc: *Heavenly Warrior*

Chief Joseph: *The Voice for Peace*

Helen Keller: *Courage in Darkness*

John F. Kennedy: *Voice of Hope*

Martin Luther King, Jr.: *A Dream of Hope*

Lewis & Clark: *Blazing a Trail West*

Abraham Lincoln: *From Pioneer to President*

Jesse Owens: *Gold Medal Hero*

Rosa Parks: *Courageous Citizen*

Pocahontas: *A Life in Two Worlds*

Jackie Robinson: *Champion for Equality*

Eleanor Roosevelt: *A Courageous Spirit*

Franklin Delano Roosevelt: *A National Hero*

Babe Ruth: *Legendary Slugger*

Sacagawea: *Crossing the Continent with Lewis & Clark*

Sitting Bull: *Great Sioux Hero*

Tecumseh: *Shooting Star of the Shawnee*

Jim Thorpe: *An Athlete for the Ages*

Harriet Tubman: *Leading the Way to Freedom*

George Washington: *An American Life*

The Wright Brothers: *First in Flight*

Malcolm X: *A Revolutionary Voice*